BONDED SHACKLE & CHAINS

LEON LITTLE

Legendary L. Leon Little

Bonded Shackle & Chains
All Rights Reserved.
Copyright © 2021 Leon Little
v1.0

The opinions expressed in this manuscript are solely the opinions of the author and do not represent the opinions or thoughts of the publisher. The author has represented and warranted full ownership and/or legal right to publish all the materials in this book.

This book may not be reproduced, transmitted, or stored in whole or in part by any means, including graphic, electronic, or mechanical without the express written consent of the publisher except in the case of brief quotations embodied in critical articles and reviews.

Legendary L. Leon Little

ISBN: 978-0-578-24032-9

Cover Photo © 2021 Leon Little. All rights reserved - used with permission.

PRINTED IN THE UNITED STATES OF AMERICA

Table of Contents

Introduction	i
1 A Conviction Culture	1
2 Banana Republic System of Justice	10
3 Shackle and Chains	19
4 Modern Day Slavery	60
5 The Big Bad Bully	69
6 Legends and Legendary	80
7 An Expensive Costume	106
8 We Should All Support Law Enforcement	121
9 Bonded	142
10 Who Made Who	155
11 Too Wrong For Too Long	165
12 My Life Matters	180
13 Dedicated to My Mom	197

Introduction

Nothing about policing in America has meaningfully changed in over 150 years. We can trace that back to policing history and the systemic oppression at the profession's core.

Early police departments are the direct descendants of slave patrol units designated to terrorize blacks, Mexicans and other people deemed by the elite class as racially interior, poor or not abiding by gender or sexual norms.

In America, the police has participated in or stood by while black people were beaten and lynched and the police has terrorized organizers of civil rights movements, peaceful protesters and/or those deemed a threat to them. The police has been known to assassinate and blackmail the less fortunate, no, not much has changed.

Racial disparities in policing and the criminal justice system are a reflection of this nation's history.

Until we figure out a way to hold these abusers accountable, we will continue to see miscarriages of justice played out in our country. Why? Until the abuse start affecting the elite of our society, there really isn't much need to change.

These elite or powerful members of our country can come up with ingenious ways to repress the poor or indigent, a perfect example is the actions carried out against me, a law abiding citizen upholding the law, but made out to be an outcast for personal and political profit and gain.

My oppressors could care less about abiding by the law because after all, they are the law.

My oppressors most likely thought they could get away with this maze of a case and no doubt thought that if the case was ever to be unraveled, who would listen and who cares.

Even being denied due process of law, discriminated against using racially charged and fabricated evidence, this group still struts about with their heads held above the poor and indigent, walking around like everything is status quo or business as usual.

Through my pen I've been given a voice and the world has provided me a platform and this book is my true story.

If my oppressors can publicly defamate and slander me, then I have a right to use their names in this book and that's exactly what I have done.

I've gathered my facts from public records while my oppressors have fabricated evidence and use trickery, lies and deception to achieve their goals. For them so far, it has worked to a tee.

As painful and as complicated as this ordeal has been for me, thanks to the Internet and my determination, I have unraveled this adventure and now I share it with you.

Chapter 1

A Conviction Culture

I AM THE third generation of descendants of freed negroes in my family, my children are the fourth generation of descendants of freed American slaves on my family tree from my Black heritage.

My great-great-grandma Virginia, they called her Maggie, was born a slave and freed from slavery through the Emancipation Proclamation later to be known as the Thirteenth Amendment. My great-grandma Mother Becky, as we called her, was 8 years old when all this took place and she gave birth to the first generation of free negroes in the family tree of my mother's heritage. That was Grandma Lillie Mae, my mother's mother.

By the time Mother Becky gave birth to my Grandma Lillie Mae, there had already been a culture mixture in America, that being Mother Becky was half Indian Black Feet Cherokee herself. The great melting pot was really heating up with the mixing and meshing of the different races and cultures in America. It's who we all really are.

I am so proud of my heritage and all the mixture of races I am, and it has all come together at the crossroads of the envitable. Everyone's story has its own uniqueness and this is my story. But, in the end it will all only prove one point, that we are all one blood and one people. That is regardless of who you are and where you are from on this earth.

I have been pushed out and pressed into a voice to bring about change into a system gone astray. I can promise you one thing, I did not volunteer for this assignment.

My own life has been scripted of storybook proportions starting on the Mississippi Delta cotton fields learning and developing family instincts, heritage and accepting innovations while making partnerships of hopes and dreams, in the new land of the free, home of the brave, and land of milk and honey.

In my personal struggles, the case I have presented before the federal courts should be of certain success whereas basic constitutional and civil rights has been violated and it's only been quieted by those who have used my life for political profit and for personal gain.

Let me break this down to you how these folks used a common negro and took themselves all the way to Washington, D.C. and at one point, John Ashcroft was considered a candidate for President of the United States.

Of course, these folks did a grand job railroading me to prison but I am here to report that the gig is up, fellas. You all deserve Oscars.

The times, they definitely have changed as a way has been provided to bring justice to a case long overdue and fought with bare necessities and uneven and unfair rules, a David and Goliath type battle where justice can be compromised for a price. Accountability is about to make a difference and about to be enforced.

If anyone is allowed to violate the rules to achieve success, then allowed to persist by using unfair illegal conduct, their margin of success will be extremely high. That is especially true in the justice system when one in a position of power and decision making options go foul of the system and cover up the facts and uses the system to their personal advantage.

There is absolutely no way that the lead prosecutor in this court case did not know that the only evidence the police presented to him was racially charged compromised material. Yet in spite of all this, these people went forward with this injustice hoping that the facts would never be uncovered and good job; its 40 years and a lifetime of suffering and disparage and the truth has finally come to light.

Without the creation of the Internet, it is very possible that this miscarriage could have gone unnoticed and that certainly wouldn't have been the first one to have. My deepest passions and prayers have and will always be for all those unjustly left hanging from the tree at the noose of the rope. I can personally and empathically feel their pain and I can feel the torture they experienced.

The initial prosecuting attorney in this case, Stephen Limbaugh jr. got the people really fired up saying stuff like he didn't care if it was his mother he'd prosecute and an ex-state trooper should know better. And of course I mostly agree with the prosecutor but this prosecutor did not mention that he was using and now proven racially charged counterfeit evidence perfectly set up and executed and carried out for 40 years now.

After Stephen Limbaugh jr. so cleverly got this case fired up, he ingeniously passed the case on to Larry Ferrell as prosecuting attorney for the Cape Girardeau Police Department. Here, both prosecutors are in violation of Rule 3.8 of the American Bar Association. When this case is passed on to Missouri Attorney General John Ashcroft, he too now joined in a conviction culture and also in violation of this Rule 3.8 of the American Bar Association.

When Stephen Limbaugh jr. passed the case to Larry Ferrell, he apparently thought I could never unravel all the pieces to the puzzle but sir, it's taken 40 years but I did it. You know sir, that the wheels of justice can turn awful slow but here's looking at you judge, let's keep the wheel churning forward.

If you don't have to follow any rules, then rules don't really matter. Rules only apply to those that have to follow them and that's apparently not everyone. The rules have especially not applied to this bunch.

In the American justice system, a rich man who is guilty has a better chance of walking out free than a poor man who is innocent. So in order to obtain any certain justice in this land of the free, you'd better be packing, wheeling and dealing.

Most often, when you're indigent and represented by a public defender, your guilt or innocence has very little bearings on how the case will resolve. It depends more on tributal issues, trade-off deals and *quid pro quo* activity.

The public defender system has sent more innocent men and women to prison, some to death row, and it appears that no one is concerned about fixing the problem because it's making too many folks too much dough.

This public defender system has created a conviction heritage and it's keeping our nation torn apart and always on the edge. What is most striking about this campaign is its seeming indifference to the lives of the people that are affected by these tragedies.

This conviction culture has become a weapon of war on the indigent, a weapon to be used by the rich and powerful, mostly when all the different political and economic strands of the heritage come together and a decision is made *ex parte* then really only one side is truly represented by counsel.

It can be political, economic or military and police pressure one thing is clear: This conviction culture is used mostly by the powerful members of our society, the people in these positions of power are forcing their will upon the public and often stealing from the public coffers all at the same time.

Until the flaws of our conviction culture are addressed, it will remain a tool of power and it's a deadly tool at that. This flawed system has consumed the lives of millions and millions. When our government does finally get involved to solve this problem, I'm almost certain that the United States of America will be dealing with war criminals as the atrocities committed against the indigent are nothing less than crimes of war.

I do have a prescription for this mess, but because of the lucrative subject nature we're dealing with, no one is willing to get involved because it could mean killing the goose who makes the golden eggs.

The first thing to do in solving this issue is to eliminate the public defender system as we know it. Give an indigent a pool of maybe five attorneys to choose from, let us call it a shark tank. Put some of the decision making into the hands of the less fortunate, the ones whose lives are being changed by these unfortunate circumstances.

Second, there have to be uncompromised body cameras worn. If an officer's camera is turned off at any point on his shift of duty, then that officer's activity has been compromised. The most ridiculous thing I ever heard of was an officer who turned off his body camera because he knew what he was about to do or say was wrong.

Third, there has to be strict accountability or this system will not work. And, of course, accountability is what will keep our system in tact and a strict scrutiny standard of review will help keep the facts clear and help keep the public involved.

In our neighborhoods we have to initiate a surveillance system of cameras; these new doorbell cameras appear to be cutting down on a lot of crime in the hoods. Develop local networks of watch and keep an eye open and you'll stay busy, I assure you.

We can do something about these issues. The question becomes when will we do something to fix the problem, or will we???

If you've ever been trapped in a situation like mine, that being railroaded to prison and freed from prison by orders of the United States Supreme Court, the excessive load and hoopla it has created, is a heavy burden to bear indeed. I can best describe the load I carry as a shackle and chain holding me back from any progress. All anyone you encounter wants to discuss is your misfortunes and your hardships, it can be really tough. It is like I'm forever bonded to this case.

As I look around at my own personal achievements, I'm left in awe because of the way the whole case transpired. These thieves and crooks are stealing my hard work and has turned it into an advantage for themselves.

Chapter 2

Banana Republic System of Justice

Upon being railroaded and sent to prison, I was astounded at the number of inmates who simply didn't have any means of communicating with their family and loved ones because these unfortunate souls couldn't read or write.

I found this out by chance as the old man cell next door told me how he paid an inmate to write letters home for him and how he had to pay another inmate to read and to interpret his mail and letters to him. He was currently accumulating even more debt, for these services and he offered to pay me to help him.

Of course, my first question was why wouldn't one guy do both jobs of reading him his mail and writing letters too, but that he said, cost extra and he already was in the hole with the many people he was dealing with. He said one inmate had provided both of those services to him but that he had gotten out.

Free of charge, I started immediately providing these services and immediately I found myself imbedded in the private lives of over half dozen inmates.

I also found myself in the middle of a turf war between the East (St. Louis) and the West (Kansas City), the Muslims and Skinheads, the Crusaders or Christians worship, very much alive and well in the penal system.

These groups believed me to be stealing their customers, and to be providing these services free was even more appalling. I suddenly found myself under attack from different angles and these thirsty devils had blood on their minds.

From my experience, once these vultures saw or tasted blood, it made them even more brutal, meaner, and more dangerous. And now, most of these guys had already acquired this taste for blood.

In prison, there's rarely a fight where there's one on

one. Most often, a gang is involved and usually it's one inmate against the gang which usually meant a gang beating. My first few encounters was against rival gangs I was lucky that none of my initial confrontations involved knives, mostly boots and knuckles and numbers against me. I survived.

In the early stages of my confinement, every prison guard wanted to see the ex-state trooper now in prison for rape. Most even wanted to chat as some even openly showed disgust towards me and verbally expressed their distaste and operated and performed their services accordingly.

For instance, every time this one particular prison guard saw me, he'd immediately pull me out and he would shake me down. He did it out of hate and disgust. He would be talking to me all crazy like and trying to manhandle me. Even after I saved the prison guard's life and most guards viewed me as an asset, this particular guard never softened his stance towards me and was always mean and showed distaste towards me. There were a lot of guards who showed empathy and were fair and understanding of circumstances as they professionally performed their jobs.

My cell was an attraction on the prison tour. I'd be

sitting in my cell and here comes a tour group mugging at me in my cell. If I didn't want to be bothered, I'd pull my curtains to. I was lucky enough to have curtains that I could pull over my cell bars which only had to be uncovered during count.

I can assure you that curtains to cover the bars, a television or a radio was not a luxury most inmates enjoyed. It was usually steel walls on three sides and those damn bars always in front of you.

Until the day of the riot did I see a bright light flash towards the end of a tunnel. I suddenly realized that there was a way out but I had a lot of darkness to defeat in order to achieve it.

Within one hour of the riot, I was summoned to a conference to an interview with a microphone. I never saw the person who was speaking to me; only a room full of cameras catching my every move from every angle and the microphone. The main answer they were seeking was why did I intervene and get off into the middle of the mayhem which I found myself involved in. I told the microphone that I simply pulled these inmates off of the prison guard in distress but when the mayhem started way off on the other side of the very newly built cafeteria, I snapped my head around to an object exploding on the newly laid cobblestone wall as several inmates had a guard pinned up against that cobblestone wall as he was slowing sliding down the wall as the life was being choked out of him. I suddenly realized that the main choker was the inmate who lived in the cell door next to me as I leaped up and knocked these inmates away from the guard. As the guard's elbow slammed to the floor, he reached for his walkie talkie with his other hand and yelled into the receiver: "Mayday!!! Mayday!!! New cafeteria!!!"

Before he could get the second Mayday out, all you could hear was the noise of keys jingling and the hoofs of boots pounding and that's how the Mayday squad entered into the cafeteria where there were dozens of desperate inmates waiting.

The riot raged for several minutes until the guards had regained control and had carried away the hostile, wounded, injured and defeated. After my initial contribution of freeing this guard's neck, I sat down back at my table and watched the whole thing unfold.

The object exploding up against the cobblestone wall drew my attention away from the riot and focused it onto a gang of inmates trying to kill a guard. The intensity and hostility was consuming most of the cafeteria as the riot squad entered the room. I would guess that close to 100 or so inmates were included in the riot and maybe close to that many guards armed and attacking anything standing up.

Even though I had said rarely a word to the inmate next cell to me, I really don't know what propelled me to get involved except that it's what I was supposed to have done by destiny. I stood in front of the cameras and spoke into the microphone within one hour after the riot.

Within days of the riot, I received a letter from the Parole Board and within a few weeks I walked out of the Parole Board meeting with newly found hope and a new mission, with an achievable out date of less than five more years and a brighter and brighter light at the end of the tunnel. Even though I had been given this new out date, I still continued battling my case all the way to the United States Supreme Court and before my case made it through to the United States Supreme Court, I was let out on parole.

Every single day that I spent in prison, that light at the end of the tunnel seemed to have gotten brighter and bigger, right up to the day I walked out of that hell hole as a somewhat free man.

The Ku Klux Klan Act of 1871 was a good step forward for the negro, but with cases like mine, where the police are allowed to break the law, miscarriages of justice are inevitable.

The Civil Rights Act of 1964 addressed the issues again but when you're allowed to miscarry justice and use the law as this outfit has, a conviction is a foregone conclusion. Of the Bill of Rights, this outfit of court officials and policemen violated almost all ten of them.

A list of constitutional rights that has been violated against me include direct violations of six of the Bill of Rights plus the Fourteenth Amendment violations.

It has been impossible for me to recover from being denied due process of law, this gang was assured of victory. It's a joke, the trial these folks held, it was more like a lynching. Yet, our constitution promises the right to a fair trial.

For as long as we continue to use a broken public defender system, the indigent will never enjoy equal protection of the law, or equal access to the law.

These criminals denied me the right to counsel, the right to confront my accusers and the right to cross-examine my accusers as they continue to hide behind the cover of the law. I am here to report that the gig is up.

The public defender system is broken and the poor and indigent are the ones who will carry the burden of fixing this vital function.

This is a two-tier system, one for the poor and one for the rich, and cannot continue as it has so far. Our justice system is a classic Banana Republic and instead of us getting closer and closer to solving the problem, it seems the problem only gets worse.

I never dreamed that our elected or even appointed officials would use our justice system to violate my constitutionally protected rights but that's exactly what Stephen Limbaugh jr. and John Ashcroft have done.

In Banana Republics, high officials sometimes pressure other officials to carry out vendettas against others to defend their friends or comrades. This is the type of activity that's been swapped around in the case at hand. When our public and elected officials use this type of activity, it is impossible to overstate the danger.

One term that Stephen Limbaugh jr. and John Ashcroft have never invoked is "the rule of law". That term refers to a government of law and not of men, i.e., our constitution. The term "the rule of law" may soon disappear from our political lexicon and we're going to miss it when it is gone.

This type of activity appears to be the undoing of American democracy.

Is America becoming a Banana Republic? The American election process should determine whether we remain a free country in the truest sense of the word or do we become a corrupt Banana Republic completely.

Chapter 3

SHACKLE AND CHAINS

THIS IS AN unbelievable case, I am still fighting for justice after 40 years.

After all my hard work and contributions as a law abiding citizen, I have been openly discriminated against and I have been denied due process of law, over and over and over again.

All extracted from court records, this book is proven police misconduct, fabricated evidence, prosecutorial misconduct, overzealous prosecuting, collusion, and extreme complicity on every level.

According to the United States Constitution, immunity does not apply to any officer who violated a constitutional right and the violated right was clearly established at the time of the violation.

Prosecutorial misconduct starting with Stephen Limbaugh jr. as prosecuting attorney for the Cape Girardeau Police Department and infesting the Missouri Attorney General's Office where Missouri Attorney General John Ashcroft became partnered into a miscarriage of justice, supporting a conviction culture where power and greed has taken control over common sense and reality, while grossly violating this citizen's constitutionally and federally protected rights.

These conspirators aided a persistent and widespread discriminating practice well settled in this case, so as to constitute a custom.

There are clear cut guidelines laid out by the American Bar Association that all attorneys have sworn to uphold. Yet, in this particular case, all of the rules have been openly violated, disregarded, pushed or set aside as was the ruling or adjudication in this case.

Rule 3.8 of the American Bar Association Rules of Professional Conduct: *requires prosecutors to make timely disclosure to the defense of all evidence or information that tends to negate the guilt of the accused or to mitigate the offense; *a prosecutor may not file in court or maintain a charge that the prosecutor knows is not supported by probable cause; *a prosecutor may not invidiously or otherwise discriminate; *a prosecutor may not intentionally avoid pursuit of evidence or information because it may damage the prosecution's case or aid the defense.

The options were clear when my case was remanded back to the lower court, to correct to retry or to set aside. The lower court chose to set aside under an Order issued by Federal Judge Stephen Limbaugh jr., now acting as a federal judge from a case he initiated as prosecuting attorney for the Cape Girardeau Police Department.

Appeals function as a process for error correction as well as a process of clarifying and interpreting the law.

Abuse of authority, abuse of discretion, multi-level misconduct, overzealous prosecuting and extreme complicity, major violations it could easily be argued that these are all gross violations.

The trial judge, Judge A.J. Seier, erred by failure to grant a motion to secure the assistance of an expert witness to aid an indigent suspect, thus rendering the trial fundamentally unfair. The trial judge also failed to allow an identification instruction to the jury and here identification was the main interest in contention. The trial judge was also a part of this injustice.

The out-of-court identification (the hypnosis) and the in-court identification of me was so unconstitutional as to assure the identification of me in any subsequent identifications. And now, the unprovoked raid upon me on December 14, 2011, 31 years later, by the Cape Girardeau Police Department was nothing short of harassment while causing severe depression.

None of these allegations were ever supported by probable cause and the only evidence the conspirators had to prosecute me was this fabricated racist and politically motivated hate evidence which was gained through prosecutorial misconduct police misbehavior and misconduct.

There was plenty of exculpatory evidence supporting my innocence: 1) the first police officer on the scene of the alleged crime Officer Susan Botinot of the Cape Girardeau Police Department who stated that the victim told her that she never saw her attacker's face; 2) crime scene fingerprints not belonging to me, the accused; 3) crime scene hair samples not belonging to me, the accused; 4) strong alibi witnesses of more than a half dozen people.

Reversible error: 1) abuse of discretion by trial judge; 2) prosecutorial misconduct; 3) the lower court ruled in an improper manner or against legal precedent; 4) not instructing a jury on the applicable law; 5) a police department destroying or omitting evidence improperly; 6) the original prosecuting attorney in this case now acting as a federal judge, injecting bias into the proceedings or appearing to do so.

Constitutional violations: 1) I was denied due process of law; 2) I was denied the right to a fair trial; 3) I was denied equal protection of the law; 4) I was denied equal access to the law; 5) I was denied the right to confront accusers; 6) I was denied the right to cross-examiner accusers; 7) I was denied effective assistance of counsel; 8) I was denied protection against unreasonable search and seizures; 9) I was denied right to pursue happiness without harassment; and 10) I have been denied protection against cruel and unusual punishment.

These are blatant and malicious violations of my civil and constitutional rights and the Cape Girardeau Police Department is liable.

I was denied due process of law and discriminated against in order to gain a conviction in Missouri v. Little, 674 S.W. 2d 541 (Mo. bac 1984). The Fifth Amendment protect rights to due process. The Fourteenth Amendment protects the right to due process of law and protects the right to equal protection. No statute of limitation protects either due process of law violations or discrimination violations however significant, this case stands alone on a case-by-case basis and I am praying that this case is treated as such.

This case is unique in the fact that it has already victoriously gone before the nine judges of the United States Supreme Court and this unusual circumstance involving this case brings us full circle with the continued activity of the Cape Girardeau Police Department, stalking me and issuing frivolous warrants.

When the Cape Girardeau Police Department is allowed to disrupt my sense of harmony over three decades later unprovoked and without probable cause arises unsettled issue and present new complications... The Fourth Amendment prohibits unreasonable search and seizure and sets out requirements for search warrants based on probable cause.

And yes, I do appeal this decision to dismiss my

civil case and pray that the Constitution is applied and I am allowed redress of grievance and my case is set for trial. I will be refiling a new civil complaint against these conspirators. The First Amendment gives me the right to petition the government for redress of grievance.

Being denied effective assistance of counsel in Missouri v. Little and a police department which fabricated evidence placed me in a position of hardship that I cannot fully recover from. Almost by a miracle, I made a decent recovery until my sense of harmony and sense of security was destroyed by the Cape Girardeau Police Department causing almost total chaos.

It is not my wish to represent this case *pro se*, but a position that has been forced upon me because of actions committed by the Cape Girardeau Police Department.

The hardships still yet compile when the Cape Girardeau Police Department is allowed to disrupt my sense of security and harmony unprovoked and over thirty years later causing stress and depression.

Discrimination in this case is a real issue that has to be addressed the way the Cape Girardeau Police

Department has violated my civil rights using techniques ruled illegal and unconstitutional by the United States Supreme Court. *Little v. Armontrout*, 835 F.2d 1240 (8th Cir. 1987) violated right to due process using fabricated racially charged evidence. There should be no statute of limitations on violations of civil rights where discrimination is involved.

This case is exactly what civil rights laws were passed to protect against. How the Cape Girardeau Police Department used racially charged evidence to make an identification of a suspect, then manage to hide most of the incriminating evidence, while the case gets lost in court. In this particular case it has been lost for almost 40 years.

To discriminate against me, the Cape Girardeau Police Department used photographs of me and a gorilla in a photographic lineup, photographic display, or photographic layout as described by the Cape Girardeau Police Department. This photographic display consisted of a set of three pictures with the second picture consisting of me alone, the space the gorilla occupied now being blank. The third photograph being blank that I occupied now with the gorilla back in the picture.

The Cape Girardeau Police Department called these photographs a photographic layout, but these photographs have no other purpose except to discriminate.

In my civil case, I presented these photographs into evidence as Exhibit #6.

Initially, *Gideon v. Wainwright* would have afforded me equal access to the courts. The denial of due process of law shifted in favor of the Cape Girardeau Police Department and a conviction was achieved. Even today, the Cape Girardeau Police Department still exercises under the assumption that it can legally arrest me, threaten and/or harass me any time and/or unprovoked.

A pattern has been established as I have been illegally searched and seized, denied due process of law, the assistance of counsel, the right to cross-examine and confrontation as so secured by constitutional amendments. The Fourth Amendment protects against unreasonable search and seizure and sets requirements for warrants based on probable cause. The Fifth Amendment protects right to due process. The Sixth Amendment protects right to a fair trial, right to confront and right to counsel. The Eighth

Amendment protects against cruel and unusual punishment. The Fourteenth Amendment protects due process and equal protection clauses.

The Cape Girardeau Police Department violated each and every right I just mentioned and Stephen Limbaugh jr. and John Ashcroft still yet strut around as if nothing illegal has transpired. No authority should be able to go contrary to the United States Constitution and hide behind the cover of the law while violating a citizen's constitutional rights as the Cape Girardeau Police Department and these conspirators have.

The Court has long recognized that when a state brings its judicial powers to bear on an indigent in a criminal proceeding, it must take steps to assure that the indigent has a fair opportunity to present his defense. *Little v. Armontrout* proved that the denial of due process was unjust to me and it should now be translated that the arrest warrant issued for my arrest on December 14, 2011 was also unjust and should stand on its own merits for sakes of a statute of limitation in which I have to respond. This principal, grounded in significant part on the Fourteenth Amendment due process guaranteed of fundamental fairness, simply as a result of his poverty, an indigent is denied the opportunity to participate meaningful in a judicial proceeding in which his liberty is at stake; this is both unfair and unjust.

The Cape Girardeau Police Department continues harassing me because first I was denied due process of law to get us to where we are today with these continued bullying tactics, threats and harassments.

An indigent is entitled the assistance of counsel at trial . . . *Gideon v. Wainwright.*

And that such assistance must be effective . . . *Evitts v. Lucey* -, U.S. – (1985); *Strickland v. Washington*, 466 U.S. – (1984); *McMann v Richardson*, 397 U.S. 759, 771, n. 14 (1970).

Before a witness may testify to an in-court identification of a suspect, the state must prove by a clear and convincing evidence that the in-court identification of the suspect has a factual basis independent of the hypnotic session. The factual basis in this particular case was the use of me and the gorilla photograph as a means to identify me in this miscarriage of justice.

The Cape Girardeau Police Department fabricated this evidence, deceived a jury, and caused a conviction. Not even the cover of the law should protect the department and its conspirators of this heinous crime committed against me. Like that of a murder, there should be no statute of limitation and it is called due process of law that I have been denied.

Poor criminal Defendants have a constitutional right to court appointed experts to counter the testimony of prosecution witnesses who have been hypnotized. My court-appointed expert was a broke and broken public defender whose only experience in the law was to bargain away an innocent man's life.

The court has ruled that it is not necessary to determine whether the victim's testimony had been reliable but only that the trial judge should have appointed an expert to help try to counter the testimony.

The Eighth United States Circuit of Appeals in this case concluded that the denial of a state provided expert on hypnosis rendered the trial fundamentally unfair.

Being denied the basic tools to put up an adequate defense rendered this trial unfair and is in direct violation of my guaranteed right according to the United States Constitution. No statute of limitation exists for a violation of constitutional rights as those involved in this case. *Little v Armontrout* is direct evidence as proof of violated due process of law.

Elements . . . conduct by a person, who acted under color of law, and proximate cause, a deprivation of federally protected rights is what this innocent man has been subjected to. The Cape Girardeau Police Department acted criminally and willfully violated my federally protected right to due process of law. Deprivation of Rights under color of law Title 18 USC Code 242 Section 14141. According to that rule, the penalty for violating this section is stiff and can even include facing the firing squad.

The fact of a state law violation does not resolve whether I have been deprived of due process, the manner in which the violation occurs as well as the consequences are crucial factors to be considered. *Missouri v. Little* is proof of fabricated racially charged evidence and denial of due process of law.

It has already been proven that I was deprived of actual constitutional rights and these rights were clearly established at the time of these violations.

The Federal Courts ruled that my rights had been violated by the Cape Girardeau Police Department, and that stigma has held me back from social advancements in society. Having to carry such a burden is very difficult to overcome. Being denied employment and coping with all the rejections, disgrace and humiliation is not easily overcome. Especially when I become the brunt of politically motivated campaigns using my case and my misfortunes as a means to further advance their personal and political causes.

It was the Cape Girardeau Police Department that reopened and revisited this issue by executing the search warrant entered as Exhibit 2 in this case I filed. With everything I had gone through, shock and confusion were suddenly back in control of my life with the execution of this search warrant.

When those officers executed that warrant on December 14, 2011, that activity also should have commenced a new period or limitation in which I had to respond to this action. For every action, there is a reaction, and this complaint is my reaction to the Cape Girardeau Police Department's actions. This complaint falls well within such limits as defined by the Court.

However, I still seek due process of law which has and continues to elude me. It is all as a direct result of the illegal activity of the Cape Girardeau Police Department.

Threats and harassment bring uncertainty into

your life when a man doesn't know whether the police can or will arrest or disrupt his life or upset and disrupt the harmony within the family. This attack is unprovoked and without probable cause bringing even more confusion and uncertainty into your life. Entered as Exhibit #2 the illegal search warrant executed against me was served without probable cause and unprovoked.

This activity by the Cape Girardeau Police Department also has a permanent effect on my wife and children bringing them unnecessary stress, pain and discomfort. Not knowing from one day to the next whether your life will be turned unnecessarily upside down is hard to cope with, especially when this attack is premeditated and unprovoked.

Stress, worry and depression have taken control of my life as a result of the assault on my character. This unprovoked attack could serve only as harassment. The stress has been tremendous, uncertain about whether these officers have a legal right to execute this warrant and whether this unanswered question could be settled in court.

Starting with the assault on my character on December 14, 2011, I began a rapid decline in health, requiring a series of therapeutic counseling sessions and a regimen of medications to help cope with the new issue presented by the Cape Girardeau Police Department. Exhibit #3 recent medical summary was entered into this civil case as evidence.

Where does the harassment end? It started with *Missouri v. Little*. That does not give the Cape Girardeau Police Department the license to ruin my life forever.

According to the United States Constitution, I have a legal right to challenge the legality of this conduct and I have initiated none of this activity but have a constitutional right to respond to the issue.

I was living under the court order of Exhibit 1, having set aside the issue at hand, but now it has been reopened and revisited upon the request of the Cape Girardeau Police Department, with the issuance of the search warrant entered as Exhibit 2 in this civil case. Exhibit 1 said this conviction had been set aside, but the Cape Girardeau Police Department can still obviously continue to stalk, bully, and harass me and threaten me with arrest for reasons not known. What is known is that this activity has been triggered by the Cape Girardeau Police Department, and this can be resolved where it started in a court of law.

The manner in which I've been denied due process of law has great significance here when we consider the nature and viciousness of the violation of due process of law against me. I did not create this case. It has been presented to us thanks to the Cape Girardeau Police Department, and the long trail of evidence it left behind with it.

The many officers involved and the evidence these officers used in order to gain a conviction has great value whereas these officers still have a vendetta against me and have made a decision to stalk and harass me unprovoked by the use of this search warrant issued on December 14, 2011. The Cape Girardeau Police Department has the authority of the law as a cover, their warrant to arrest me was simply renewed and continued, unprovoked assault on my character and harassment. The evidence now called Exhibit 2 in the civil case has its own merits and this evidence was handed to me by the Cape Girardeau Police Department. There was no probable cause supporting issuing such a warrant.

In spite of me making every effort to recover from

this hardship presented to me in life, on December 14, 2011, and over thirty years later the Cape Girardeau Police Department reopened this old case by raiding me at my place of employment, thus causing an uncertain future and severe emotional distress.

Probable cause did not exist back then nor does it exist now for the Cape Girardeau Police Department to interrupt my life with these bullying tactics, threats and harassments.

I had made a nice recovery in life, even after having been denied good employment because of the excessive luggage of having been incarcerated. I had worked the last 19.9 years as a factory supervisor at a business which was one business separated from the Brentwood, Missouri, Police Department.

At approximately 9:30am on December 14, 2011, I was raided at my place of employment by two Cape Girardeau Police Department officers and three Brentwood, Missouri, Police Department officers. My pleading of general agency in my civil suit places a name and a badge number on all of the raiding officers.

The main issue presented now is the unprovoked raid upon me on December 14, 2011 by the Cape

Girardeau Police Department. However, the past abuse of my constitutional and civil rights supports my assertions that this latest arrest of me by the Cape Girardeau Police Department was nothing more than an unprovoked assault on my character and harassment. The initial confrontation with the Cape Girardeau Police Department, *Missouri v. Little*, is crucial as collaborating evidence in this new unprovoked attack on my right to be unrestricted in freedom and life from repression. It's like dragging around a ball and chain everywhere you go.

With this raid on December 14, 2011, the officer as always carries the authority of the law so when the Cape Girardeau Police Department officer said that I had only got off on a technicality, knowing what took place prior, I was fearful of reincarceration. Now I am asserting that this raid by the Cape Girardeau Police Department has its own merit and this activity is in violation of my constitutionally protected rights.

The fear of reincarceration was real on December 14, 2011. These officers had a search warrant. More scrutiny should be placed on the issuance of this arrest warrant rather than denying me access to the court.

I've been in total distress every day since the police

raid on December 14, 2011. I have not been able to work a single day since the day these officers raided me at work and this attack was unprovoked and without probable cause.

I cannot stop thinking about the first encounter with these officers in 1981 and the almost 40 years that have followed. I currently have firsthand knowledge how these officers can fabricate evidence and change a man's life forever. *Missouri v. Little*; *Little v. Armontrout* is proof.

In the thirty one years after prison, I enjoyed freedom from repression, I had found a decent job and a great wife. Together we had two children ages 11 and 13 when this unprovoked raid interrupted my life. This attack on me has been very stressful on the wife and children. This attack is not only unfair to me but to them as well. I also had older children and now grandchildren that have suffered emotionally as a direct result of these miscarriages of justice toward me.

Starting with the raid on December 14, 2011, my health has gone in a downward spiral, as a direct result of this attack on me by the Cape Girardeau Police Department.

This book is part of my response to the raid upon me by the Cape Girardeau Police Department and these facts should stand on its own merit as a commencement date of a new statute of limitation in which I have a right to respond and should not be tied to any of the original proceedings except as collaborating and supporting evidence.

This response falls well within a statute of limitation inconsistent with the right of due process of law which, according to the United States Constitution, has no statute of limitation. These conspirators left behind a mountain of evidence and a pile of corruption and violations and abuse.

The manner in which the Cape Girardeau Police Department used racially charged evidence to gain a conviction sheds light on why a statute of limitation should not apply to this case. No official or authority should be able to use racially charged evidence of any nature to gain a conviction, then to be able to hide behind the cover of the law as a shield.

I believe the court has refused to address the evidence used to convict me but a trial is going to expose the heinousness of these offenses and these violations should be characterized as hate crimes. This evidence supports these assertions. *Missouri v. Little. Little v. Armontrout.*

It is also apparent that this federal judge has erred by first not affording a citizen the right to seek redress and by not accepting this character's assassination of me as a legitimate concern of the court. These same issues have required federal court rulings prior and all the way to the Supreme Court. I assert that the violations have not changed and the violations continue until I have been afforded the constitutional right of due process of law.

All past activity has highlighted the attack upon my character on December 14, 2011 but as a citizen with constitutional rights, I have a right to challenge this present unprovoked conduct of the Cape Girardeau Police Department directed toward me, with the execution of the search warrant.

This federal judge stated in this background summary that the police officers raiding my job site on December 14, 2011 was "apparently investigating a rape". The background in this particular case has all the evidence to support that this brazen move on behalf of the Cape Girardeau Police Department to reopen this case, was nothing short of harassment and unlawful detainment. Each and every case should be on its own merits and on a case-by-case basis.

Exhibit 1 sets the aggression of the Cape Girardeau Police Department aside until further time as the department decided to react upon me again. The Cape Girardeau Police Department decided to re-act upon me again on December 14, 2011. I have every right to respond to this harassment and this response falls well within a limitation as so required by the court.

This was an illegal search and seizure and no probable cause exists to continue treating me criminally, nor did any evidence ever exist to treat me unconstitutionally.

Starting with this warrant executed against me on December 14, 2011, and entered as Exhibit 2, these present and past actions against me have been a violation of my constitutional rights and are contrast to privileged granted to all citizens. To rule that I have no right to challenge this unprovoked and questionable conduct is itself now my challenge.

The issue involving discrimination will be addressed as these officers have used fabricated racially charged evidence in order to make an identification of a suspect. Of what other purpose could the Cape

Girardeau Police Department have used the picture of me and the gorilla except to discriminate? The use of me and the gorilla photograph in the identification of me as a rapist so violated my rights as to guarantee a conviction. This comparison of me with the gorilla used in the manner in which the Cape Girardeau Police Department used it, guaranteed that the choice of the subject under hypnosis would be me. Every single witness who testified at trial in *Missouri v. Little* had been hypnotized by the Cape Girardeau Police Department hypnotist, B.J. Lincecum. The Cape Girardeau Police Department has presented a classic case of discrimination to this court and it is an issue the court has to consider.

The actions by the Cape Girardeau Police Department of recognizing me as different so much that I was treated inhumanly and degraded is a violation of my constitutional rights. For violating a citizen's due process of law, there is no statute of limitation to hide behind.

In the thirty one years that I was free from incarceration, employment was often hard but not impossible, to obtain whereas the interview goes well right up until the potential employer discovers you spent over six years in prison. That stigma developed into a source of oppression for me and has created social hardships causing undo stress and emotional discomfort. The police raid on December 14, 2011 was more pressure than I could handle, not certain about my future with this new problem presented to me by the Cape Girardeau Police Department.

Enduring the discomfort I did find gainful employment working two jobs to help care for my family for ten years until being disrupted by the Cape Girardeau Police Department executing a search warrant against me hurling threats and totally disrupting my state of harmony and my sense of security.

I have every legal right to challenge this conduct, or do I???

The federal court has acknowledged that my rights were violated years ago and that violation of my rights was due process of law.

Oops!!! There it is…

This case will survive a strict scrutiny standard of review whereas fundamental constitutional rights have been infringed, particularly those found in the Bill of Rights and those that the Court has deemed a fundamental right protected by the due process clause of the Fourteenth Amendment. These infringements violated explicit constitutional protections, burdened fundamental rights and access to the courts and other rights recognized as fundamental, i.e., equal protection and equal access.

We have clear and gross violations of my civil, federal and constitutionally protected rights. Every person who, under color of any statute, ordinance, regulation, custom or usage, of any state or territory, or the District of Columbia, subjects, or cause to be subjected, any citizen of the United States or other person within the jurisdiction thereof to the deprivation of any rights, privileges or immunities secured by the Constitution and laws, shall be liable to the party injured in an action at law, suit inequity, or other proper proceedings for redress.

The Cape Girardeau Police Department clearly violated my established constitutional rights and acted in a grossly unreasonable fashion. These actions were taken with deliberate indifference and racist intent and Cape Girardeau Police Department is liable. Cape Girardeau Police Department has left behind a trail of incriminating evidence so great that only the strength and power they possess as law men has protected them to this point. These are the kind of lawless acts that the civil right acts were meant to eliminate. However, by using the cover of our law, unfortunately these acts often recur.

Clothed with the authority of the law, the Cape Girardeau Police Department and conspirators intentionally misused the power entrusted to them and maliciously and willfully violated my civil, constitutional and federally protected rights.

The United States Constitution, Fifth Amendment's due process clause requires the United States government to practice equal protection. The Fourteenth Amendment's equal protection clause requires states to practice equal protection . . . Thus, the equal protection clause is crucial to the protection of civil rights.

Discrimination may be so unjustifiable as to be volatile of due process.

Civil rights guarantee equal protection under the law. When civil rights are not guaranteed to all as part of equal protection of laws, or when such guarantees exist on paper but not respected in practice, opposition and legal actions, even social unrest, may ensue.

It was gross negligence on behalf of the Court to

reject my request to provide assistance to an indigent party. Then again, the Court denied a motion by me to enter an instruction to the jury on identification. Here, identification was the main issue in dispute.

I have suffered nothing less than a domestic terrorist attack from the Cape Girardeau Police Department. This unprovoked attack upon me was premeditated, politically motivated violence, perpetrated against a non-combative target. It was the use of violence and threats of violence in pursuit of political and social objectives.

Basic fundamental rights protect individuals from excesses of the state, among other things they include the right to a fair trial and freedom from discrimination.

Running out the clock: With this fabricated evidence and misconduct toward me, these officers caused excessive charges to accumulate at every level, exhausting every state and federal court and to the United States Supreme Court twice, before being defeated and admonished. John Ashcroft should be ashamed of himself for pushing this case forward but instead, Ashcroft has been honored and rewarded for this questionable activity.

Running out the clock as termed in the legal profession as these police officers caused the opposition to run up huge charges to the public all while using racially charged fabricated evidence and police misconduct.

All these charges and fees were paid to prosecute me but I was not allowed equal access to the law or equal protection under the law, clear violations, as the Cape Girardeau Police Department exhausted, every state and federal court and to the United States Supreme Court twice, where this bunch was defeated and admonished. Especially now, John Ashcroft who has by now taken over the case personally and taken it to Washington, D.C. to the United States Supreme Court, where he was defeated.

Charges exacerbated and blown out of proportion all while pushing forward an agenda which consisted of proven racially charged fabricated evidence and proven police misconduct.

Due process will require these conspirators to show accountability for over 40 years of fraudulent legal expenses, and 40 years of deprivation and corruptions.

The Order from the Federal Court unconditionally freeing me from custody is a farce and a possible violation of due process as Stephen Limbaugh jr. plays multiple roles here.

Especially notice that this Order is signed by Judge Stephen Limbaugh who initially prosecuted this case as State's Attorney for the Cape Girardeau Police Department. All the evidence used to prosecute me was fabricated by the Cape Girardeau Police Department and all the compromised evidence grossly violated my civil rights.

By signing this Order, Judge Limbaugh played roles on both sides of the aisles in this case, which I believe is unconstitutional or at least it violates rules of civil conduct, or conduct of common law.

The Order signed between Judge Limbaugh and the agreement between him and the now prosecuting attorney to retry or not to retry the case is possible collusion and possibly a violation of my civil rights. Judge Limbaugh admits in the Order that he had contacted the Cape Girardeau Prosecuting Office but recusal by Judge Limbaugh would have been more appropriate here.

Even at this early stage in this case, Judge Limbaugh signing this Order is to be disputed and this judge should have recused himself right here, now acting as a federal judge, thus exposing his role as the initial prosecuting attorney in this case but that did not transpire right here.

Recusal of a judge should be based on a matter; the matter presented here is a judge playing roles on both sides of the aisle and whether these roles interfere with due process of law. A major attempt to diminish my case is reborn here by Judge Stephen Limbaugh jr.

After living 31 years of freedom, peaceful co-existence and reconstructive lifestyle, trying to recover some dignity and honor, on December 14, 2011, uncertainty invaded my life as the Cape Girardeau Police Department drove 125 miles one way to once again disrupt any hope in the pursuit of happiness coveted by me when the Cape Girardeau Police Department interrupted me at my place of employment about 9:30am executing a warrant against me claiming that I had only been released from custody on a technicality and that made the search warrant that they held valid. This search warrant is entered in my civil suit as Exhibit 2.

Afraid and confused on December 14, 2011, again I experienced shock, depression and fear and this uncertainty has made me fearful and petrified of future contact and harassment from the Cape Girardeau Police Department, who has threatened my life and pursuit of happiness now as REPEAT OFFENDERS.

A partial medical history exposes the mental depression and anxiety caused by these conspirators. This medical report is entered in my civil suit as Exhibit 3.

On August 13, 2015, I filed a motion in federal court seeking redress from these conspirators. However, this complaint was dismissed out of Judge Limbaugh's office as frivolous. Out of Judge Limbaugh's office – COME ON MAN! – do you really believe it is legal or constitutional for Limbaugh to still be dealing with this case in any manner? A copy of that court receiving and filing that complaint is entered as Exhibit 4 in my civil suit.

Again, Judge Limbaugh had an opportunity to recuse himself but it was not until I filed this a second complaint and two years later until Judge Limbaugh recuses himself. By now, his bias and influence in this case hints toward a strong case of collusion and complicity. This order and the order of dismissal are entered as Exhibit 5 in my civil suit.

By invading my privacy on December 14, 2011, with this search warrant entered as Exhibit 2, the

Cape Girardeau Police Department violated the order entered as Exhibit 1 and the harassment of the Cape Girardeau Police Department on December 14, 2011 violated the order and exposes them, the Cape Girardeau Police Department to this miscarriage of justice and violation of my rights.

I believe that the court order entered by Stephen Limbaugh jr. as Exhibit 1 was a shifty court move and possibly in violation of my right to due process of law.

Due process essentially guarantees that a party will receive a fundamentally fair, orderly and just judicial proceeding. Exactly the opposite has transpired in this situation.

Having continuously suffered emotional stress since the invasion from the Cape Girardeau Police Department, the depression and anxiety I suffer is great. The Cape Girardeau Police Department is the cause of this stress.

Procedural due process constitutionally requires the federal government to afford a citizen the opportunity to be heard. Up to this point, I have not been given due process and I am seeking redress.

An unbiased tribunal

The right to know opposing evidence
The right to cross examine witnesses
The right to be represented by counsel

I have not had fair treatment through the normal judicial system and this unfair process is in violation of this citizen's entitlement under the United States Constitution. This unfair treatment has been orchestrated, fabricated, and administered by the Cape Girardeau Police Department and co-conspirators, and I am seeking redress.

The Cape Girardeau Police Department has acted recklessly and with callous indifference toward an innocent citizen, with deliberate conduct that shocks the conscience or offends the community's sense of fair play and decency.

The use of the photographic display, photographic line-up or the hypnotically induced evidence is fabricated by the Cape Girardeau Police Department and the invasion and continued harassments from the Cape Girardeau Police Department should end here and now.

The obvious graphic display of conduct on behalf of the Cape Girardeau Police Department is offensive to everyone except for when it is the law who violated the law, sometimes it's almost impossible to achieve justice.

The picture of me and the gorilla is now entered as Exhibit 6 in my civil suit. These photographs are marked stamped and dated by the Cape Girardeau Police Department and several months prior to the Cape Girardeau Police Department arresting me.

These photographs are simply an example of the bungling efforts of the Cape Girardeau Police Department trying to cover up their conduct. However, time has unraveled all the evidence and it's all been created and fabricated by the Cape Girardeau Police Department.

Using *Leatrice Little* case, it's also amazing that a prosecuting attorney Stephen Limbaugh jr. can parlay his job into a place on the federal court using this phony racially charged evidence but not only that then a state's attorney general John Ashcroft can parlay his job into the position of the Attorney General of the United States of America. All while pushing forward this corrupt case and taking it twice to the United States Supreme Court where this bunch of violators was busted, defeated and admonished.

This is the type of conduct that supports my

charges of civil and constitutional rights and due process violations in this case.

After I was used by prosecuting attorney Stephen Limbaugh to secure an elected position by razzing me publicly and obviously using corrupt racially charged evidence, former prosecuting attorney Limbaugh was elected as a federal judge. Then Stephen Limbaugh passed the case on to Larry Ferrell as prosecuting attorney, who used the racially charged illegal evidence to gain a conviction. Then, Farrell passed the case on to the State's Attorney General's office featuring its star jurist Missouri Attorney General John Ashcroft, who used the case and phony evidence to prosecute the case up to the United States Supreme Court where these violators were busted and the case was overturned and reversed.

Here we have a strong case for collusion and complicity as well as due process violation and I am seeking redress.

These actions are questionable and I believe an investigation of this case is necessary. I reached out to the United States Department of Justice to put them on notice of this civil rights lawsuit. The Justice Department reached out to me and the response of the United States Department of Justice is now entered as Exhibit 7 in my federal civil suit.

The Department of Justice investigates crimes and not individuals. The decision to investigate should be made on the law and facts and on a case-by-case basis.

The civil rights violations by persons acting under color of law is apparent in this case. The violations against me will prove in a court of law or trial to be hate crimes all with evidence the Cape Girardeau Police Department and conspirators have provided for us and left behind. This evidence will prove to be extremely racially charged and this fabricated evidence was absolutely the only evidence the conspirators had to prosecute me. When a police officer appears in a court room and points his finger at you, it is very hard to overcome.

These conspirators may be held criminally liable for a federal felony or misdemeanor, if they conspired with the government to commit actions which violate due process clauses of the United States Constitution.

Can the violations in this case be made any more clear? The trail of evidence that these conspirators has amassed is overwhelming, beyond a reasonable doubt and only the arrogance and power of the conspirators have kept a lid on this cover-up for this long period of time. I have almost lived 40 years in fear of the Cape Girardeau Police Department and now I hope to finally settle in court this dispute.

The emotional roller coaster I have experienced over the last 40 years is extremely taxing on the body. I have suffered severe depression and anxiety as a result of this whole affair.

The Cape Girardeau Police Department provided the prosecuting attorney's office racially charged fraudulent evidence to deprive a citizen of his fundamental rights. All of these officials knew exactly what they were doing. To profit from the affair included a prosecuting attorney who overzealously prosecutes and a federal judge then an attorney general, all overzealously prosecuting. All this activity transpired on the pretense of racially charged and fabricated evidence and police misconduct as the opposition sparred no expense to the public and all while depriving a citizen equal protection or equal access to the law.

John Ashcroft, being Attorney General of Missouri, then of the United States, gained national attention around this state and Washington, D.C. as a hard-nosed jurist. Yet, John Ashcroft used the *Leatrice Little* case featuring extremely racist evidence to help to facilitate his hard-nosed stance. This is a fact which was proven in the United States Supreme Court where this scheme was exposed and busted.

Running out the clock while an innocent man is left to deal with the consequences, overzealously prosecuting and using compromised racially charged evidence proven illegal and obviously corrupt.

The late great Senator John McCain took notice of Attorney General John Ashcroft's behavior and the only living sitting senator in America ever to appear on *Saturday Night Live* made a special guest appearance on the famous television comedy show. In a skit on the *Saturday Night Live* show, Senator John McCain portrayed United States Attorney General John Ashcroft.

The skit Senator McCain played was very funny on the one hand but on the other hand, I felt humiliated and scorned having personally been the scuttle of Attorney General Ashcroft's amusement. I do not have the power or authority to present before the Court a copy of the broadcast of the *Saturday Night Live* broadcast without copyright violations. However, the Court has the power and authority to request such a recording by accepting this portrayal of Attorney General John Ashcroft's role on the show as federal evidence in a civil rights suit.

The skit from the *Saturday Night Live* broadcast is entered as Exhibit 8 in the civil suit.

Thank you, Senator John McCain, for your service and commitment to this nation.

This case was nothing short of a modern day lynching. All the facts and all the evidence hint toward a racially charged hate crime.

Other supporting evidence includes a list of 12 or more physicians that have treated me for depression over the last nine or so years and a more comprehensive medical report in more detail, personal witnesses, former employers including potential former employers who denied me employment because of this case and this harassment.

The list of witnesses also includes several people that were with me 100 miles away from this crime scene, at the time this alleged crime was to have transpired.

The list of witnesses also includes hostile witnesses like then jail administrator Namad Ackers, then Sheriff Boyer, then Deputy Sheriff Tim Wright, then Cape Girardeau Police Department detective Bill McHughes, and then Cape Girardeau Police Department officer Susan Botinot.

I pray that a strict scrutiny standard of review is applied to this case and that this case is advanced forward and readied for a trial.

In good faith I submitted this evidence in support of my petition to hold the conspirators liable and accountable for their police misbehavior and criminal conduct.

Applying the strict scrutiny standard of review will prove that this case is worthy of having shown many serious violations, on a civil, state and federal level, enough evidence supports this case to bring it before a jury.

Chapter 4

Modern Day Slavery

Man slave has been extremely successful and very profitable here in America and for that matter, probably since the origin of man.

This exercise is humiliating and demonizing while bringing riches to an elite class usually repressing and denying people their civil and human rights.

To cover up for this terrible repression, the elite has come up with different ways to disguise this torture like the Jim Crow Act of separate but equal, apartheid, and secretly training your children to not mingle with the negro in public while at home teaching them to treat them as second class people.

Let's be straight about this: the racist has unjustly and even criminally repressed the less fortunate mostly negro especially male, by violent and abusive acts often arresting and charging them with frivolous and unsubstantiated even fabricated offenses.

Our jails and prisons are packed with these poor souls often because the system has been stacked against them from the very beginning.

An experience of this nature can change a man's life forever and has a big impact on his future and on the man's family and loved ones.

Until now, there has never been much regard for the families' loved ones and friends of these people, but recent movements have brought more focus on this problem and have opened the eyes of many who were unaware or blinded and oblivious to the issue.

This problem is an old issue but movements now have placed a seriousness on trying to do something to fix or at least talking about the core of the problem which is long overdue.

These reckless exploits have had a bearing on how black parents have reared their children. In my family, for instance, the very year I was conceived and within miles of my home, a black child named Emmitt Till was lynched and killed by a mob and the mob has been shielded from prosecution by the law or those feeling like they're justified, superior, or has a right to carry out this type of abuse for whatever reason they wanna.

No one ever stood before a court to answer for these crimes even though everyone, mostly everyone, knew who the perpetrators were.

I've personally been touched by these acts of aggression, not just my own miscarriage of justice and railroading to prison, but as a child, my daddy took me to the home of a man who had been hung to death by these vultures. My dad and the elders had a name for these vultures. They called them the beast. I didn't always understand it but I heard my daddy say it often to other adults in their conversations, "Well, the beast struck again last night."

My dad held my seven-year-old hand tightly as he used his other hand to pull the sheet back from over the deceased head, where I saw a sight that has lived with me since.

My parents often emphasized and preached to me not to ever look at a white person, especially a woman. If one walked toward you, the best thing to do was to look down as you passed them, turn around, or to walk to the other side of the street. As a youth in Mississippi, I witnessed white women often flirting with colored men, trying to gain attention, causing trouble, and not caring what the outcome would be.

Looking directly at a white person was a very serious offense back then. My Uncle Bobby was lynched and left for dead for whistling at a woman. Somehow Uncle Bobby lived to tell us about his howling experience. All he could remember about the white woman was how pretty her long flowing red hair had grabbed his attention and almost costed him his life.

To the dismay of many, instead of being prosecuted for their crimes, a lot have been cheered and celebrated as they carry on like they're better than everyone else. But new light has begun to shine on these acts and even though they are lessening, they still yet continue to be perpetrated against the poor and less fortunate.

Often the police, law enforcers, or the ones who are supposed to be upholding the law, are the ones committing these crimes.

Even though Emmitt Till was murdered 65 years

ago, the perpetrators or even maybe the relatives of the perpetrators have gone back to Emmitt's grave site and have damaged or destroyed the tomb.

These racists have often done their dirty deeds in the open public, but the cries for justice have dampened their boldness and have forced many to commit these acts under cover of darkness again.

In some cases, their mask has been removed. The faces of the evil have been exposed.

These exposed criminals have tried to hide behind the church and the Bible a lot, because there's no way these atrocities could have gone on for so long without the help of the preacher and the church. When using the Bible and church started failing them, these criminals have used the cover of the law with cold manipulation, calculation and control. They invade your home and your privacy under the law, they hanged and shot us under the law and they unjustly incarcerated us under the law.

It has been extremely hard to carry on except for a small chance, a glimmer of hope, and a prayer. But most importantly, it has been the dream that has carried us on.

Hope has allowed us to dream and the dream has

guided us to a promise. The promise has been written in a constitution and shared by a nation.

My prayer is that the promise will be indivisible under God and restored to greatness and to enlighten and to restore the dream.

I'm not living the dream, as to many these days may say when asked, "how you doing?". So many are oblivious to all the pain, suffering and torture that has gone into them being able to speak those words. I'm living the dream.

I too actually thought I was living the dream until I was abducted in broad daylight, openly lynched in our court system, and used for personal, political profit and gain.

Most often, when the racist has taken an indigent or colored person's freedom or his life, they come up with any kind of dirt they can on the person to justify what they've done to them. In my case, there's no dirt to uncover because I've given a life of service to this country. First, as an 18-year-old enlisting in the Marine Corps during the Vietnam era while men were abandoning their country or simply refusing to honor it. After that service call I returned back home and became the eighth black man to become a Missouri

State Trooper. So they can dig on because there's not a lot they could come up with except that this was a modern day lynching and it's been like I'm simply just a modern day slave.

You know, I didn't set out to become a writer but with my education I always had the ability to do some writing. American history has always intrigued me. In fact, I probably took an overdose of it in my college studies. With that knowledge and my unfortunate miscarriage of justice, it was easy to translate my words into a book which became published as *When the Law Corrupts*.

Even with my good knowledge of history, I was weak in law but I've always upheld the law and represented the law on levels that have been unprecedented, honored and respected. To me, that only goes to show that it doesn't matter who you are to the racist it's all about that skin tone, or the color of your skin.

That has to change and is most stupid but a change in mindset has to change first. A normal functioning mind should see a person, a human being and a sister or brother and a child of God.

In America, we need to kill the racist idea and resolve to the beginning and the beginning is right here and right now. We need to make the American justice system a place of real equality, real fairness and real integrity. We need to restore the promise and make it a place where there really is justice for all.

It's been real clever how my little bunch of clumsy racist has managed to hide my unjust in plain view while making millions in revenue for themselves and their cronies. These guys have managed to distort the American justice system for profit while destroying hopes and dreams and ruining values unprecedently but I really do now believe that the gig is over and a new day has dawned. I don't have to name the whole bunch of you my pleading of general agency places a name and number on all of you and I'm here now to report that this gig is up.

For over 30 years I've toiled in your darkness just dreaming of justice one day. So when you came back looking for another pay day from your disgusting little dirty deed, I hardened and fought back and now here my fourth book is out about your little filthy encounter I've had with you. I won't be your slave any longer.

From our first confrontation until you came back calling, a very unique thing happened, it was the invention of the Internet that gave me a tool to study and a tool to research and now these telephone cameras are exposing your dirty deeds all over the world. It's now time for you to start to worry. The times they are a-changing. Your modern day slave is exposing you fellows as modern day racists.

I have so much gratitude to the internet for helping me to conceive the unconceivable, to believe the unbelievable, and to achieve the unachievable. But my work is long from being done.

Chapter 5

THE BIG BAD BULLY

IF YOU HAVE ever been bullied, then you can probably share my pain, as I've lived 40 years of my life being dominated by a powerful force using tricks, lies and deception to keep you silent and under control.

A bully is one who domineers by insolence or threats or they overbear with bluster and menace. It is too simple for our police to be bullies in America and change is overdue.

The intimidation from the bully can change one's life and in some cases, this pressure has cause catastrophic and detrimental harm towards its recipients.

The challenges we'll face in life are often hard

enough on an every day occurrence dealing with each other in society, but when our police becomes the bully, life can become complicated.

With advancements in technology using mobile cameras and such, we can actually capture many instances of police bully tactics but when the bully uses our court system to do its dirty work, it can take years even decades to detect its menace.

A bully is one who is habitually cruel, insulting or threatening to others who are weaker, smaller or in some way vulnerable. If you treat someone in a cruel or threatening or aggressive fashion, you are a bully. To abuse, brutalize, ill treat, ill use, kick around, manhandle or to mess over someone simply because you're able to do so, you are a bully.

I have been bullied by the Cape Girardeau Police Department. This outfit used the justice system to achieve these ends.

A bully is one whose strength and courage are based on the intimidation of those who are weaker.

A mean person or group or organization who hurt in anyway is a bully. Because I was bullied by the Cape Girardeau Police Department, writing this book is really painful as I relived the traumatic experience I've been forced to live through.

Bullying someone most likely leaves behind emotional, mental and sometimes physical scars and can influence your life forever.

Bullies are scum, pure and simple. They torment people who can't defend themselves and they revel in the suffering of innocent people who never did anything to hurt them.

Bullies are the reason for the Colombine shootings and are a big part in why bad things happen to people, including why people commit suicide.

When a person stands up for himself or herself, the true nature of the bully will often show as a cowardly and spineless worm. During most of my early childhood, I was influenced by the bully. As a child, I had no one to look after my best interest even though I had three older brothers. Often I was bullied by them too except for my very oldest brother who I believe was a gift from God. But he couldn't look after me. He moved away from the family once we moved to Missouri when I was eight years old. The main core of the family settled in Southeast Missouri, but my two oldest brothers didn't stop there with us, thinking that they would have a better chance in St. Louis.

Even though my older brothers did not look out for

me as a youth, I made an early decision that I would do everything I could to try to protect my younger brothers. I had four younger brothers and stayed busy in the ghetto making sure I protected them so they never had to experience what I had to.

One of the worst bullies I encountered in my neighborhood was about seven or eight years older than me. This guy went on to play professional football, coached by the legendary Vince Lombardi. This guy often came back home during the off-season and roamed the ghetto selling cocaine. He eventually died from its use at an early age, broke, desolate and near homeless.

Drug use has taken the lives of so many of my friends in my peer group, most at a very early age. One of the biggest and hardest problems I face as a parent is trying to keep my kids away from drugs and not giving in to peer pressure.

Another bully I was influenced by was a group of four older boys, maybe three to four years older. As a group they would chase you down and beat you down, but one on one they were weak and cowardly. One on one I'd beat them like a drum even two of them on one I'd beat. But there wasn't much I could do with them when they were together except maybe get in a good shot or two and take the whipping they had for me. But after they'd beat me, I'd seek them out individually and I would whip them like Muhammad Ali whipped Joe Frazier twice.

One of those chumps tried that bully crap on me after I came back home after I served a stint in the Marines and he became the first man I ever knocked out cold. It was with a body punch to the chest, left hook. I thought I had crushed his chest plate as he lay there on the ground gasping for air. He's been humble since that left hook put him on the ground. Even today almost 45 years later, I make sure I keep that chump in check and I don't have to remind him of that thunder I displayed that day. The coward threatened to shoot me if I ever hit him like that again. But I've never had to because apparently that punch did what I needed it to do, sent him a strong message. I'm not the one you might want to push around.

In my life, I've never been the one to pick on people and I often defended those in need if I was able to. In some ways I owe the bully a debt of thanks. Because of them I got tough and when I was bullied by the Cape Girardeau Police Department and railroaded to prison, I wasn't shoved around in prison because I had long since learned how to stand up for myself. I fought back and I fought back hard. I had thunder in my hands.

In prison I was called the sledgehammer after I was jumped on by this guy who had robbed a bank in my hometown and was serving life+50 after he kidnapped and murdered a bank teller. He said g—damn, that m----- f----- hit like a sledgehammer and that's the nickname I carried with me during my incarceration.

Early on in my incarceration, I was beat by a gang and I was beat at one point beyond recognition. But those cowards knew not to test me heads up and they were trying to recruit me into their gang by group intimidation and fear. Even with the beating, I refused to join the gang. I faced those cowards every day for my first year behind the walls in Jefferson City, Missouri. Then I was transferred out to a medium security prison, but only for a short period before I found myself back behind those walls.

One inmate behind those walls tried to make me his bitch and he reached up and put his hand around my neck, trying to choke me. Bad mistake. I grabbed his arm and broke it in 16 different places. I really wanted to twist his arm until it fell off but after it snapped 16 different times, I let him go. I know it popped 16 times because the group of people who gathered around to watch counted each pop. The first guy said "oh shit, he broke it", then they counted each pop all the way up to 16, where I let him go. By the time I got to the 16th pop, there was a large group gathered and all were counting. It sounded like a choir as we got to the 16th pop. Amazingly, the prison administrator placed this man back in my unit when he got back from the hospital wearing a full arm cast.

About a month after that incident, this fool came back after me and I kindly broke his arm again, this time he was put in another unit. I never saw him again. With his good hand the chump had a knife and he stabbed me. He also stabbed a prison guard before he was overpowered. If I ever do see him again, I may have to hurt him again, unless his attitude has changed, I may be forced to.

Another inmate claimed he was a karate expert. He jumped up and kicked at me, but I grabbed his foot and twisted and broke his ankle, when I slammed him to the floor, he broke his toe. After that he was extremely humble and when I'd see him out on the prison yard, hopping around, all he could say was, "He broke my toe, he broke my toe". The last I ever heard of this inmate was where I read that he'd done something bad and that he had been put on death row.

I was lucky that the fights I had didn't result in more serious injury to me even though I was stabbed and gang beat while I was incarcerated. I had a lot of fistacuff fights but these clowns didn't know, nor did I, that I was protected by angels. There's no other explanation I have, how I managed to survive those walls in Jefferson City, Missouri.

It took guts to even walk into the gym behind those walls. It's where a lot of men lost their lives. This is the same gym that former world heavyweight champion Sonny Liston pumped iron. His mural was painted on those walls. But I walked in there and I went over to the basketball court and said, "I got the next game." One clown looked at me and said, "what?" and I said again, "I got the next."

Other inmates sat up in the bleachers and watched the show because this was no ordinary game of basketball. It was a game of rough house. Unfortunately, for one inmate who tried to tackle me as I made a steal and headed back the other way toward the basket, he tried to pull a stunt as I went in for the lay-up but my elbow caught him on the forehead above his eye. He came back from the hospital with 22 stitches in his head. I thought he would bleed to death before he got to the hospital, I was afraid. But this was really an accident on my part. I wasn't trying to hurt him and after that incident I looked him up and apologized to him for that incident. He accepted my apology but wouldn't play ball with me anymore.

I'm going to end this chapter talking about how much I dislike bullies. I hate them a lot. I've often stuck my nose into other people's affairs if I saw someone being bullied.

I don't mean to sound mean or act tough, but I have always had all my sisters backs like that and if their old men don't like that then that's their problem. They all know who I am, they know my reputation.

I once heard that one of my six sisters old man had given her a black eye so I drove 600 miles round trip to talk to him about that situation. When I got there, her eye looked all normal but I told her, with him standing right there, to just tell me that the joker had hit her. But she said that everyone was alright. She wouldn't even confess that the joker had ever hit her. I wanted his ass and I asked sis if this chump had ever hit her. She loved this clown and wouldn't confess that the clown had ever hit her.

Of course, he got upset and asked me if we could talk in private. I did agree to go out to talk with him, but before we did, I told my sister that if this guy ever hit her to just tell me so. When we got outside, all he wanted to do was talk. I had on my cowboy boots, I had put them on especially for him, and I really wanted to bury my boot off in his behind but the chump wouldn't give me that chance.

When we got outside, I told the chump that if sis ever called me that I would be back. The chump packed up their stuff and hauled him and my sister back to his hometown in San Antonio, Texas, thinking he would get her down there and treat her any way he wanted. But after a very short period, sis got tired of his crap and called me, asking me to come down, get a U-haul, and to bring her back to Missouri. Before I could make those arrangements, one of my brothers flew down there, rented the U-haul, and brought sis back home.

The chump followed her back to Missouri, but sis

had had enough of him. She never gave him another chance even though the chump stalked and begged my sister until he realized that sis had someone in her corner that had her back. This clown stalked and begged my sister for over ten years until she finally succumbed to her illness and died of cancer. The chump then packed up his junk and moved back to Texas.

I became like that about sis after I grew up because sis proved her worth to me as a youth. When I was 10 or 11 years old, two guys chased me into the house where sis was. Sis went outside and kicked their butts.

As a child growing up, if I needed someone to take care of a bully, it was sis who answered the call. Even though sis was small in stature, she had guts and fought for me against men in the hood. Some bullies didn't mess with me because they knew I could call on my tiny big sister to defend me. While most kids would call on an older brother to defend, it was my little big sister I often called on. My big sister was no joke and no one, I mean no one, ever fought harder for me.

God knows I still miss my sister and I pray every day that she's gliding around heaven and still taking care of business. Sis… I will always love you and I never ever knew I could ever miss anyone so much.

Chapter 6

———∽∽———

LEGENDS AND LEGENDARY

HANDED DOWN BY tradition; inscription; story; myth; mythical; fabulous. Self portrait of a legend.

Whenever we talk about any subject, the best or most famous often rises to the top in conversation, leaving others to awe at their achievements to marvel at or exploit their accomplishments.

For example, when you're talking about professional boxing, most often the name Muhammad Ali comes up, because his fights have become legendary in the sport of boxing. Back in the day when Ali fought, the whole world seem to stop, watch and wonder as we all listened to a new promise today and looked toward a better tomorrow.

In my city of St. Louis, Missouri, if you speak of great or famous sports announcers, the names Harry Carey, Jack Buck, and Mike Shannon will often enter the conversation because these men have become legends in their fields of studies.

Most recently, Joe Buck has been enshrined into the Hall of Fame where he now joins his legendary father. This might be the only father and son combination every enshrined into the Hall of Fame.

When Harry Carey worked in St. Louis and early on in Chicago, during a game broadcast, if he yelled, "There's a line drive!!", it was often followed with a "Holy Cow!". But toward the end of Carey's career, he often fringed the edge of his chair on every ball the Cubs hit out of the infield. No baseball announcer kept more fans entertained at a ball park than Carey as they often watched sub par baseball as the national crown evaded the Chicago Cubs for around 100 years. Carey was as big a part or more at keeping fans pouring into Wrigley Field, and now good baseball is back and the Windy City thrives.

When Jack Buck told folks to "Go crazy folks,

go crazy!", he etched his voice as legendary as those words resonate, and a new baseball dynasty thrived in the Midwest, easily surpassing old attendance records with crowds unheard of challenging all records and having great success, as St. Louis, Missouri, fringes on the verge of dynasty.

For me personally, when I met Muhammad Ali in the flesh, I stood in awe and just stared at the man from about ten yards away, for well over an hour before being dragged away by my wife, while I complained the whole way and stared at him until he was out of sight. I was mesmerized by the man's mere presence, as I watched him sign hundreds of autographs, as there was no end to the line in sight.

Not only was Ali a great boxer, he was the only negro I ever knew who won a case in the United States Supreme Court. As I stood there and stared at the great Ali, I am almost sure other guests probably thought I was some type of security guard for him. I just stood there and watched the legend who by now was only a shell of the great fighter he once was. As I watched the great Ali sign these autographs, I wondered how he could sign them the way his hand and body shook and carried on, being riddled with Alzheimers.

When I met Harry Carey, I thought I was seeing things as he appeared right in front of me wearing a camouflaged desert type floppy hat and carrying a backpack. Harry said, "How you doin' buddy?" as he walked unescorted in front of Wrigley Field in Chicago. When he moved to Chicago, he then became a legend there. Those words still resonate through my mind, "How you doin' buddy?". I think Harry said that to just about every one he met. The seventh inning stretch is legendary in Chicago with Harry's voice gruffling through the ballpark speakers as the greatest baseball fans in America cheered on the song and waved as they sang *Take Me Out to the Crowd.*

I enjoyed my personal experience watching and listening to these legends as I was held captive as a hostage by the State of Missouri and city of Cape Girardeau, Missouri, as an injustice unfolded, while these great voices inspired me on as we each were carving our niches in a society, and we each left our mark on our communities.

As I listened to these great voices, this legendary story was still being developed. The United States Supreme Court eventually freed an innocent man from prison and gave this case a stamp of approval and enshrining this event as unbelievable and a legend to be remembered.

Making of the legend takes time to develop as the special talented ones inspire us and motivate and push us forward.

When Harry Carey left his job in St. Louis, I personally though St. Louis could never replace the wonderful talent but then again time has a way of producing legends as the great Jack Buck and Mike Shannon entered my life and made the loss of Carey fade fast. Buck and Shannon energized and inspired me through the worst period in my life. While the voices of Buck and Shannon swelled the ball park, crowds in Cardinals Nation now challenged the Windy City as champions of the greatest fans of baseball in America. Yet unbeknownst to me, my life too was on a road toward legendary.

When I met Carey in Chicago, I said, "Harry, we miss you in St. Louis." At that period, the legend was in the making but the process not quite complete, as events continued to unfold making fans while leaving imprints and etching places in out hearts and our lives.

I felt the presence of Shannon and Buck, as I sat

in a jail cell in Jefferson City, Missouri, and wondered if I would survive to hear those voices again tomorrow, as day by day you endure, leaving behind trails of accomplishments and a story, which will be talked about and celebrated forever.

In my mind, I can hear my grandchild or great-grandchild saying, "Yes, grandpa did spend time in prison but he was freed from prison by orders of the United States Supreme Court."

Gaining my freedom through the United States Supreme Court was gratifying for me but being denied my right to protest this injustice has motivated me into writing my fourth book pushing forward my agenda and leaving my mark behind. Others will marvel over or wonder how such an injustice has been allowed to transpire, as my work in life takes its twists and turns all while writing a story and leaving a mark.

Even before my victory in the United States Supreme Court, my service to my state and country has been epic both locally and nationally, as I became an elite United States Marine rapid deployment force member or soldier and only the eighth black man to become a state trooper in my state, leaving behind a mark that can never be challenged, and accomplishments that can never be taken away. As a United States Marine, my fellow soldiers called me Poster Boy. As a state rod, my co-workers called me the 8th or 8th Wonder, referring to the fact that I was only the eighth one of my kind. Some even called me Super Trooper.

As an elite force Marine, I often wondered why all this exercise as the whole force was up every morning, and before 6 o'clock we had already run several miles. Being ready when called was part of the job as we were always ready. And our rapid deployment was apparent as our advanced unit deployed and destroyed the Cambodia Navy, sinking three of its four ships in one hour and freeing our spy ship the USS Mayaguez which was being held without cause. The force is an American legend.

After I was released from jail, the trailblazing would go on as I took up the game of golf in 1987 and made new friends as we challenged each other for acceptance as equals, and made unbelievable shots on the golf courses and stories we passed on to others who probably thought the stories themselves were also unbelievable.

For instance, the time I played a match to the

18th hole and I was carrying a two stroke lead, until my competitor made a hole-in-one par 3 to even the match, and create a sudden death shootout, which ended by darkness as dead level even. The match is talked about today as the story is passed on from grandfather to son to grandson and to the awestruck listeners, whose all ears has turned to make sure that they hear the great story. Now when the subject of golf comes up, I'm reminded of the great match.

For me to even get onto the golf course was special because at that period in our history, a black golfer was not something you saw every day in St. Louis. I didn't let that deter me as I looked for playing partners and broke through the walls of resistance and became a fixture on the public golf courses of St. Louis, respected as a good golfer and competitor. I found my first set of golf clubs in the trash. I went to a practice range and worked out for hours after work every day before I felt good enough to go out to a golf course.

My most indelible memory is having the white golfers seek me as a partner, and I go on to lead the team to the championship as I hoisted the trophy cup in victory and won the DIMAC golf open in 1998 in St. Louis. I finally broke through the barriers restricting the game of golf to more than just a color issue, tearing down walls of resistance at my work place and setting precedence and changing the old way of doing things.

After I won the DIMAC open, co-workers who once refused to play alongside of me suddenly wanted me to play on their team as a partner and new friendships developed and old ideas abandoned.

After that victory I was even invited to play golf on a lot of private courses in St. Louis as many looked at me and wondered who the hell is that negro. To me, leading and setting an example of excellence is always my goal and in whatever type of endeavor I enter, I strive to do it better than it's ever been done before, then I push every time out to even improve upon my accomplishments, always challenging myself even after it's no competition, now you're just challenging and pushing yourself.

After my release from prison, that's how I pushed myself on my last job in the business world as I entered the Dow Jones stock market in about 1995-96. Starting from zero, I pushed my company to develop a 401k savings plan and within one year, my investments were the most prolific in the whole company minus the owners of the company, who made huge salaries and lived like kings. I started barely above minimum wage and I worked my way up to one of the highest paid factory workers all within five years. Hard work.

When the Cape Girardeau Police Department forced me away from my job, I was the most powerful employee in the whole company. I was known as the hardest working man in the whole company of about 100 employees. Before the police forced me away from my job, I also had the most progressive investment plans, as I was about to enter my 20th year of employment. I had worked so hard to get back after being let out of prison. Even the owners of my company came to me for production information as the supervision out within the factory left a lot to be desired. Most of them, the other supervisors, were simply overcome by greed in my opinion. None of those supervisors will have anything negative to say about me because I really was the hardest working man in the whole company and I carried them all.

In the line of production, I learned everything there was about the company to know and I used this knowledge to propel me to the top, as supervisors came to me seeking information and bosses and owners came to me always wanting more.

On December 14, 2011, when the Cape Girardeau Police Department showed up on my job, it was 31 years since my release from prison. I had pushed an account from zero to right at 150 grand.

On good days I could make 10 grand or more on the Dow, and on bad days I lost 10 grand.

Had the Cape Girardeau Police Department not interfered in my life after obviously stalking me, I would have enjoyed the growth the market has seen today, August 2020, and my account would be worth well over a million bucks and even so much more. I believe this police department knew these figures after careful and considerable stalking, and decided to strike me again to see if they could continue to cause me more pain and grief, thus further violating my civil rights with frivolous warrants only issued under fraudulent complains and made up evidence.

The magic number for my stock account to strike one million bucks was about 18000 points. Today's market is way above that which leaves me to wonder further why me then why me again. But then again that just introduced a new weapon into the game as I won't go away, and I'm determined to make my voice be heard and my prayers be answered.

Before I was incarcerated and after I had resigned from the Missouri State Highway Patrol, I had a heavenly type vision as I was frightened but made to be calm as a premonition appeared and consumed me and ordered me to hold on tight for an experience I was about to endure and one I would never forget.

Hell yes, I was afraid and at that point I had no clue what when where or why.

It was late summer and just a few months before I would be abducted and held captive for 6.3 years, before being freed by the United States Supreme Court but the struggle was really only starting with my release from jail. I moseyed on blazing that trail I had started, making plans, making history and changing lives. Mostly it was the change my life was about to embark upon: A life in a world of violence and violence like you'd see in a war but the weapons used are hand to hand combat, utilizing knives, razors, nails or any concealed weapon that you could get your hands on in prison.

I was broadsided by a corrupt force and I found myself locked up in jail and that's when I realized what the premonition was all about as a spirit appeared in my jail cell, whom I thought was the angel of death, but when he passed me over, I felt a calmness and I knew I would survive that ordeal.

The rest is history as my case went to the Supreme Court victoriously but still denied my civil rights as a force uses its power to retard my life and invade it upon its request or demand.

That's part of the road to becoming the legend I guess, as I keep pushing this pencil to dullness, then I sharpen its point for more, as I suddenly realize I have a story to tell to the world. Now this pencil has become one of my dearest friends and trusted allies.

Back in 1967 when they bussed those white students into our school, the ghetto dudes used that to strike fear and pain into the lives of the innocent white students and upon any colored student who socialized or talked to a white student. But I endured the abuse as I crossed color barriers and fought for cooperation between the races. It was no easy task, but my vision was clearly coming into focus. The legend was in training.

Nothing could stop me from raising my hand for my country during the Vietnam War because I wanted to be part of the progress and part of the change.

Our boys were winning the war but everyday news cast was ended with a count of the dead, wounded or injured. Change was going on but the road to change was not exactly clear.

After the Marine, I raised my hand to my state as I continued my trailblazing, witnessing the worst school bus accident in the state as little children laid with severed arms or faces, and a drunk driver walks away with his life as moms and dads woke up to the nightmare, Little Johnny won't be coming home no more.

I found myself on the morning of the bus accident facing this horrifying tragedy spaced out and in another world. I felt the pain of the Kelly School District parents and others' great loss that day, as I directed emergency vehicles in and out and kept an open lane into and out of the accident scene. It all felt like a dream. At the same time, I was keeping away spectators, some no doubt had loved ones in the crash but now they could only get in the way if allowed into the scene. There were already more than enough volunteers on the scene, those who had gotten there before the scene could be taped off.

Emergency vehicles and helicopters rushed in and

out while news choppers tried to get good aerial shots. I thought we could have an air collision, the air traffic was so thick on that foggy fall morning near Sikeston, Missouri.

That night at home as I viewed the newscast, most were wondering who was the black trooper down there, while friends and loved ones called me on the phone and talked about LL being on television that night. I suddenly felt out of place and in a thick fog.

Even though I had a great job, in reality I knew my life was meant to be more than that of a policeman, working all the accidents, hauling folks away to jail, writing all the tickets, all painful and guilt ridden. I really felt bad as I wrote up my uncle and next door neighbor, but speed kills, I told them, and Uncle Frank, your license will be suspended again, this is your third offense for DWI, no, I can't let you go.

As an alternative job, I would often daydream of a career in the Marine Corps or playing pro baseball. A few years prior I entered a spring training camp for the Cincinnati Reds. I had visions of playing catcher and dreaming to bench and replace the legendary one, Johnny Bench himself. No doubt only a dream because Bench now resides in the Baseball Hall of Fame forever but in my mind, he was simply holding a place I should have acquired.

I wasn't one of the ones scouts drooled over. That day in spring training there was a big lefty hurling strikes in the bullpen. I was catching his fast ball, which made my glove pop and my hand hurt. Hey, that one reached 100 mph I heard one scout say, as he pointed a jug gun at every pitch Tim threw. They were all over him and he went on to star in the majors for several teams, but I was invited back for another look at another spring training camp.

I didn't give them a second look and joined the Marines instead. But at 16 years old I had big dreams, as I dreamed of my service and heeled the call of the United States Marine Corp at 18 years old.

We have designated those to speak for us as elected leaders or spokespersons, but to me too many voices remain silent, while leaders assume personal goals as corruption and greed has been allowed to invade our system. That leaves me to speak out against the corrupt policeman, crooked politician, or those on the take as a code of loyalty prevents other officers from standing up for justice. I refuse to stay silent and I advocate for those who didn't have a voice.

I personally wanted to be more than one who always represented taking away from others. I wanted to be a giver and not a taker. I found no happiness in my job as a state trooper only and always issuing out pain or bad news to someone, so I packed my bags and moved on.

In so many ways I often thought I was being targeted because I moved on but I soon realized I had wondered into a racist front yard and the job of lynching a negro was a great rush and a great challenge. With all the money and all the power, the lynch job was a given.

They almost got away with it but the trail left behind is so obvious as position, power and politics continue propping up a racist whose time has run out. All the facts are still in place and some day soon, they'll be re-examined as the picture of the negro and the gorilla lay in the archives, knowing the day will come when they'll be called back into service and that bigotry will be exposed. The last big showing of the negro and the gorilla was to the nine judges of the United States Supreme Court who viewed them and set an innocent man free. You would've though that was good news but fact is, it has so far only propped up a puppet and violated an innocent man's civil rights and ruined his life.

But the court's ruling angered the corrupt force who refused to loosen its grip and stalk and harass me forever any time and at its request. That's a privilege you enjoy if you're the rich and powerful as you keep your hand buried off into the public trusts and making god-like rulings. And you keep your knee firmly placed on the innocent's neck.

But that angered me and led to my filing suit which was dismissed as frivolous. Amazing, have you seen this complaint? You could have called it a lot of things but to call it frivolous is more than stupid, and it's more than trifling and way more than petty. This was the ruling issued out by federal judge Stephen Limbaugh jr., who should have not even been involved in this case any longer.

The facts to this case are there, I didn't make them and they have not changed. It's only a matter of time before the corrupt are brought to justice.

Routes leading to my reparation were not scripted by me. Otherwise, this case would long ago have been resolved. But had they been resolved back then, I would have probably missed my chance to becoming a writer, a job I have come to treasure, as it helps soothe my mind and calm my soul.

I am sure it wasn't sportscaster Hall of Famer Jack Buck's idea to sell his beloved puppy to five different owners as the first thing Jack Buck did was train the dog how to find its way home if it ever got lost. I've heard young Mr. Buck used the money he got from the repeated sale of the dog to buy his way into the ballpark to see the St. Louis Cardinals play baseball where he was no doubt inspired by the likes of Vin Scully, Mel Allen and the legendary Red Barber.

Empathetically, I feel the pain of Emmitt Till, Travon Martin, Michael Brown, Alton Sterling, George Floyd, Breonna Taylor, almost a new name every day, and all those innocent ones left hanging from the tree, all these martyrs have left behind a mark.

We all walk through different paths towards reaching our goals, some are pleasant routes while some are violent routes and often involve you giving up your life. But being remembered post-humorously brings some recognition to an accomplishment inspiring others to take up your cause and pass on the torch.

There were many left hanging from a tree: Those are the silent voices who have entrusted others to speak up for them and to carry on the torch for righteousness. Can you hear me now, I'm now speaking out through my pen!!

But imagine being able to enjoy this life as a living legend. I am reminded of Black Jack Johnson, Charley Pride, Jackie Robinson, Buck O'Neil and Satchel Paige – all trailblazing and legendary figures in our lives who lived this life as living legends knowing they're leading, changing and making history.

Now that the voices of legends have been mostly silenced, it's the stroke of the pen that will make them live on influencing us and others to greatness. It truly is a hard job to do when you seek to do it better than it's ever been done before.

What makes all these characters legends is the lives they've lived and the stories they all have to tell. That's what life's all about – is who has the greatest story to tell and who is the first to tell that story. Then, can anyone tell that story better, or can anyone else be called the greatest one to ever do it, making history, setting records, and changing the courses of history.

Black Jack Johnson was not just a great boxer, he also crossed color barriers by dating whomever he wanted. He was also one of the first American negros to own an automobile around the turn of the century. This invention would later take Black Jack Johnson's life as he often drove his cars as fast as he could in transit.

One of my most clear thoughts of Black Jack Johnson's driving record is of him being pulled over for speeding as he drove through a town and he was levied a $50 fine. Black Jack Johnson handed the officer a $100 bill and said to keep the change, because he would be coming back going the same speed.

Speed would eventually take Black Jack Johnson's life. He finally did crash his car and died as a result of the wreck.

When Jackie Robinson broke the color barrier in baseball, he suddenly became the legend. Colored boys could now dream of playing in the bigs. Baseball became a passion and a way of life for them.

Thanks to great visionaries like Pride, Robinson, Mays, Aaron, O'Neil, Johnson and Paige, the trail has become more traveled, and opportunities have become more readily just.

You'd be truly amazed at some of the stories as to what led a particular individual to follow a certain path towards becoming the legend. But time has pushed us forward and God's hand has no doubt guided us along the way in my life for example as the racist really treated the negro so harshly and so often their only motivational reason was to push forward an agenda of hate and discrimination. It's sad but true as all the pain and suffering has gotten us to a bargaining table and real progress is being made and equality is inevitable.

Imagine this, a boy from Mississippi named Charley Pride could have been the one who broke through baseball colored barriers. However, baseball failed him and he became a legendary country music singer and the colored man's breakthrough in the field of country music. Imagine that. A boy from Mississippi.

As a new graduate from boot camp and on my way back to Camp Pendleton to report for duty, I boarded the plane and headed back to the Golden State. As I got to the first class section, I had to almost beg or push my way through the aisle as white folk crowded into the tiny area of the colored gentleman, all with cameras and chatter and big smiles. So crowded in fact that I didn't even recognize who the man was they were all abuzz about.

I took my seat two sections from the first class

section and kept watching all the excitement, but I was unable to see who it was. The airline stewardess pulled the curtain in front of me making it even more difficult to see who it was causing all the fuss. But the curtains kept flopping open and shut, and every time the curtains opened the passengers didn't give the celebrity any time to recover before the next one came in. All I could see underneath the curtain was the flash of the camera or hear the chatter coming out from first class.

It did finally quiet down about halfway through the two hour flight and the curtain flew open and the colored celebrity looked me smack straight in the face. Well, kiss an angel good morning, that's Charley Pride up there causing all that fuss.

When we got to San Diego and got off the plane, I caught up to Charley and walked with him through the airport and later on that night, there's ole Charley singing his songs on the television.

As I walked side by side with Mr. Pride, I wanted to just touch the legend but at 18 years old and a new U.S. Marine, I was too embarrassed to do that. What I didn't know is that I was walking alongside a legend and that I was a legend in the making. Imagine that, two boys from Mississippi.

I never dreamed I would have been so unjustly treated by my own nation but I am sharp enough to realize a nation is composed of people and people are not perfect.

It would have been easy to be angry for what has happened to me, but that could only complicate the issue and cause me more pain and grief. I could have been mad but the 6.3 years served to calm me down and it gave me time to figure out a plan on how to deal with the problem.

Every time I figure out a way around my personal setback, my foe seems to come up with another way to disrupt my life or another angle to use, to keep me repressed or without. And it's so amazing that these violations are always ruled legal tactic used, but in reality these infractions are real violations of my civil rights. It's like I haven't earned or that I don't deserve any civil or human rights.

That's alright though, because in my dream I had, you know when the angel came through my jail cell, I felt the power of the spirit and I know everything is going to be alright because I am simply and merely an instruments of the Lord. The sooner we each individually realize that we're merely instruments on a mission for the Lord, the world will be a better place for all of us to live.

I have got to speak for the masses who have had their voices taken away for whatever reason. Even though my own voice has been attempted silenced, my pen now has to speak for me, and all the silent voices who have been unjustly quieted, waiting for someone special to come along to carry on the cause, pushing an agenda of justice, fairness, civil and human rights.

Well, here I am, I stand before you now as that voice. Some have even called me Legendary Leon Little.

Much work has been done but we've gotten too comfortable as the racist and supremacist hate, keep corrupting our great nation.

As we keep tearing down these walls of resistance, I'd like to see them replaced with cooperation, peace and love. I believe that's what most honest people want to see.

But as long as we continue to allow obvious signs of racism, for example, my case, where a conviction is allowed to happen with racist and fabricated evidence, and even with admitting to this fabricated evidence being fabricated, a civil case is dismissed as frivolous. I am getting better in my search for justice whereas every motion I now file has been like a road map of knowledge. I feel more comfortable with each motion I file.

Yes, the legend is still in the making.

Chapter 7

An Expensive Costume

When I resigned from the Highway Patrol, shortly after I relocated to Cape Girardeau to attend the university, I attended a big party, a big celebration of some sort and bash. I don't even know who sponsored the event. Some type of pageant was also going on and it was a big gathering.

Well anyway, out of nowhere a gorilla appeared from behind me and the outfit he wore was so good that my first instincts was to run because I thought that it was a real gorilla. It sort of shook me at first . . .

When I realized it was a prank and the creature kept following me, a photographer snapped a few pictures of us. The gorilla kept following me and pranking with me then he moved on to his next subject. I kept watching the gorilla even as he joked with other guests and I swear his acts and movements were that of Bill McHughes, the Cape Girardeau policeman.

I haven't discarded the fact that it could have even been Club Foot, the cadet who was released from my academy class because the physical activity became too much to bear. This cadet had a close relative who was hypnotized by Cape Girardeau Police Officer B.J. Lincecum and this relative was a witness to testify in court.

On the morning that the Cape Girardeau Police Department came onto the campus to arrest me, Keith Abernathy, this cadet, was with these officers. He told me to stay calm. If I didn't do what they were arresting me for, everything would be okay.

This photo was used to frame and convict an innocent man and its frame will continue to arouse the public because when the picture is taken out of the archives and revealed to the public, then all will see how a corrupt force can mislead a victim, deceive a jury and public, and railroad an innocent man to prison.

I have often wondered about who was the man

inside that gorilla costume and I am almost certain that it was the police officer Bill McHughes. He fit that costume almost to a tee and as I watched him railroad me to prison, his characteristics and movements again corresponded to the same person who occupied that costume that night at that big party.

I have also had a dream that it was McHughes in that costume and to me, it indicates that I was stalked before I was framed and railroaded to prison. What kind of violation is that?

Someone knows who was in that outfit and I believe a very expensive gorilla costume resides in the Cape Girardeau Police Department supply room, or at one point, this department had ownership of such an outfit. This gorilla outfit may have also been owned by the campus police whom one of those cops had a personal vendetta against me accusing me of being the reason he could not complete Missouri State Highway Patrol Academy. He was exposed at having a club foot and came to me daily asking me to keep the pace down during our physical activity. I had absolutely nothing to do with him being exposed. It was later revealed that they were already onto him. But he was angry at me and promised that if I ever came to Cape Girardeau, he would have something for me.

But like a lot of the evidence from my case, it seems to have no problem at disappearing. I'm sure the costume is gone.

Let's remember that this has not been my will, how things have transpired and I never sat out to become the legend, but choice over time has gotten us to this point, and I won't rest until this case has been resolved, and the public official racists are exposed.

That's a pretty good one though, a small town corrupt cop uses a gorilla costume to help convict and send an innocent man to prison.

The victim in this case told the police she never saw her attacker's face, but this guy with the gorilla suit convinces her that he knows who it was. Then successfully program her through hypnosis to believe that it's the man standing next to the gorilla in this photograph he has. The only other option for me is that this was a total hoax and that there never was a crime committed at all, which means that not only did the police lie but the "victim" lied as well. All shameful and corrupt.

Imagine this, you have just been violated and you

didn't see who it was that did it. But the police tell you that they know who it was because they saw him run away from the building, we would have caught him but he ran too fast. Then more lies and more lies until you're convinced the police has the right man, so you appear at a police lineup, then in court, and point at an innocent man.

We all want to believe our police but when hate, bigotry and racism are involved, justice most likely won't be served.

Entrapment is classic in my case and the reversal of this case by the United States Supreme Court not only proves entrapment this court also reversed this case because of the unconstitutional civil rights violations.

Then for the police to stalk and harass this innocent man for decades because they're hollering, "you only got off on a technicality," is a gross continued violation of my civil and constitutional rights.

Showing up on my job after 31 years of humiliation and disrespect caused me great grief because I thought that the ordeal was far behind me.

All my co-workers were abuss with chatter as the law surrounded the building showing up with officers from several local municipalities. Three officers from Brentwood accompanied two Cape Girardeau police into my place of employment this day but the area is also served by Maplewood, Richmond Heights, Clayton, Ladue and Webster Groves. All buzzing about hoping I would try to run from them. I felt certain they were going to kidnap me again and take me hostage like they had 31 years earlier. I could only see gloom. Suddenly, I felt like I was back in that tunnel again.

The Cape Girardeau police were yelling at me that I was going to pay because I had only been let loose through fault but they failed to acknowledge it was their fault that this case even existed in the first place. It's my fault that I haven't pursued this issue more aggressively, barring excuses, I still had to go on trying to live my life. I had been rejected by every lawyer I had contacted. It seemed like I had no recourse in the matter so I got me a job and I went back to work. I kept looking for legal help unsuccessfully.

Should I have to keep a watchful eye out for the Cape Girardeau Police Department who has a knack for showing up without cause, inflicting grief and pain into the life of a man who has given so much yet has been treated so wrongly.

All this exists because a small town police got clever and came up with a way to entrap, frame and railroad an innocent man to prison. The whole gang eventually got in on the payday as they rode the case as far as they could before the piggy bank was broken.

That costume keeps racing through my mind. I believe it would have been a key piece of evidence in this case. But who owned or occupied the gorilla suit never came up in my defense because after all, I was represented by a public defender who proved in court that his office wasn't capable of giving me a fair trial, even though he knew I was innocent. It was his beliefs that I should accept a five year deal offered by the prosecuting attorney. You are facing life in prison, you know, he told me. With the time you've already served, you can walk out of here with the deal, right now as a free man, he said. You never have to go to the pen in Jefferson City, he said.

Alternately, the costume could have been owned by the university where the party was but then if that's true, then surely the university knows who occupied the costume the night the photograph was taken of me and the gorilla. I believe the person wearing that outfit is a key figure in this ordeal but until now, who this person is, has never been challenged. The other person in that costume could have been old Club Foot who returned back to the university and resumed his job as campus security officer.

This ordeal started with the gorilla costume and had continued to evolve as the show unfolded. As the public trial proceeded against me, it was like a theatrical performance as these people wore their best suits, jewelry and giddy-ups to court each day. I can assure you that it was not a play for me as I defended my life against these racists as they gloated and created an atmosphere where their victory was almost certainly at hand.

I did try to talk to my public defender about the costume but his budget and his concerns were on a more primitive level, he told me he couldn't even defend my basic rights, let alone to investigate any other claim, his budget was too tight. But once again, these incompetent cops leave behind the most crucial piece of evidence. . . <u>the photograph</u>.

This little guy, my public defender's attire, especially his shoes I noticed was always worn and scuff looking. It always looked like he'd just come in off the trail. He looked like this through all my hearings, even through my first trial that ended in a hung jury. At my first trial the public defender wore a wool suit that looked like he had been sleeping with a kitty cat. But on re-trial I noticed that even this little scruff attorney and everyone even the prosecuting attorney and victim, all had on new looking outfits and new jewelry, and now on retrial this victim had gained confidence and would boldly point at me in court, as the show unfolded, and the injustice transpired.

As this show of a trial moved on and after they had deceived a jury into believing this lie, as I waited to be shipped to the pen, an escape from custody took place right in front of me as the inmate pointing the gun told me to get my stuff; we're outta here. I could not believe I was now witnessing a real live jail break as two whites being held for murder raced past me and headed for freedom.

I simply told them that even though it looked dark and gloomy for me, I had to stay there and fight this, now my only hope was through the appeal process. I still had to stay and fight even facing a dark future as I tried to look forward. There was only darkness and gloom way out through a narrow opening, that opening I can best describe as a tunnel.

After a couple days, they recaptured the escapees and placed the white guys back into their jail cells. The guards beat the heck out of Lewis Rogers and left him hanging from a jail cell with one cuff attached to the highest bar as the negro hung there and bled for hours.

This ordeal had started with a very expensive gorilla costume and had progressed to a very elaborate display of showmanship and disgrace, as I was paraded around, shackled and in chains, and showcased as a rapist. But in my mind, I knew somehow and some way, this would all be okay someday because after all the hardships and all the pains, this has only made me stronger and it has further bronzed my life as I walk in unchartered footsteps and pave a way toward progress and change.

As this ordeal did transpire, I often thought about all the innocent this outfit had robbed of its rights. All the lives this outfit had unjustly taken, they all raced through my mind as racism is deep and cultivated in these neck of the woods as hate lives and breeds in this part of my state.

The city of Cape Girardeau, Missouri, is rich in history of torture and abuse of our civil and human rights. These abuses have been well documented and openly boasted of, but when I came to this area I truly thought we'd gotten past these ills but the power of hate fosters certain coves and hideouts I believe societal eyes are becoming focused on these atrocities and the public, I believe, will act upon them more aggressively in the future wherever they are as we continue in our efforts for real progress and for real changes.

As to date, hate has taken up the largest part of American culture. It continues to consume our society and exploit our resources.

As the city of Cape Girardeau, Missouri, continues its legacy, being one of the last cities in Missouri to hold a slave auction along the banks of the mighty Mississippi River, the case of the negro and the gorilla continues to soothe the hate of the racist of the area as it also provides a strong platform for human and civil rights. Even this mecca of hate will fade into conformity as the story continues shaping and blazing a trail while making and changing history.

With all the hurt over the years together we've worked towards a partnership which has given so much rise to promise and change.

It's a crying shame a police is the one responsible

for perpetrating hurt and pain when they come up with clever schemes to torture an innocent man, like using an expensive costume to violate and ruin an innocent man's life or a show of force to outright take a man's life, unjustly shooting or maiming them, or letting them rot away in prison, for a crime they did not commit. But, oh Lord, forgive me, because I can't ever get out of my mind all those martyrs left hanging at the tree.

I often wonder what was going through the minds of the United States Supreme Court judges as they looked at the photo lineup or photo display, as it was described by the Cape Girardeau Police Department.

The mind game manipulation's evidence had mostly been destroyed by the Cape Girardeau Police Department but its trail of stupidity is public record and will be there for review forever.

The hypnosis was merely a con game and the conviction a formality once all the witnesses had been hypnotized and they all pointed towards me. I walked around as a doomed man but I refused to give up hope, I kept my chin tilted up and I never once gave up on the dream.

I could have escaped that night after I'd been

convicted as Lewis Rogers overpowered the sheriff's department guard and took his weapon. As I refused to go, I heard their stomping across the top of the building as they fled. Going with them meant I had given up hope on a future life of freedom. I wouldn't have had the honor of having in my life gifts from God that enriched my life once I was released from jail.

Had I gone with them, I had a cousin living only two blocks from the jail and there I could have gotten a car and the gun. But I would have by then chose death if I had run and I knew this battle I fought would be awfully painful and awfully slow. Oh hell yes, I was angry enough to run and mad enough to end it all right then and there. But I knew there were greater plans in the works for me. And here I am 40 years later, still fighting for my civil, social and human rights.

I knew better to choose life over death. Escaping with them meant I would always be on the run, then it would have been easy for the Cape Girardeau Police Department to say we knew he was a criminal all the time, just look at what he just done.

Facing the dark challenge, I stood firm and fought,

not looking forward to what lay ahead or the tremendous hardships my life would for sure encounter. Every day I kept fighting and day by day I endured.

The Cape Girardeau Police Department had gone on a witch hunt and it found its prey, an innocent black man, and now I felt the stones of society pelting at my body as the events unfolded and I walked through the gutters of humanity as a marked man.

Even living down in the pits, I always felt the presence of the holy spirit as I walked. There was an aurora of my life shadowing me, like I was always in a dream and I was looking down on me as I lived day by day.

I've come to realize that it was the spirit of the Lord sheltering me, guiding and leading me because there's no way one man could or should have done all the things this one man has done in this one lifetime.

It seems to me that the goal of us all should be to have an honest police force but when the integrity of our police is the subject, everyone wants to label you as anti-police. It's almost like a certain level of corruption is acceptable and these abuses are normal everyday occurrences. You've heard this a lot . . . accountability, the buck stops here.

I guess it will be normal as long as we continue to

allow corruption on a level of this scope, and no accountability is being applied to control the chaos.

No, I'm not challenging the police but I'm challenging corrupt behavior by the police and this should be a cause and concern for anyone who loves the law and for all who love our great nation.

Chapter 8

We Should All Support Law Enforcement

Law enforcement is a key function in our country and it's a very important element to having a smooth running society and economy. Law enforcement in America has seen so much change and through law enforcement the underprivileged have been able to help bring forth this change as more and more minorities are filling the ranks of our law enforcement.

Law enforcers shouldn't be feared by the public, but certain elements have penetrated law enforcement ranks and these pirates have taken on a personal agenda putting themselves above the law and then wreaking havoc on the underprivileged.

A prime example of this is the police officer arresting a young black man who's not resisting but cooperating with the arresting officer, yet the suspect is slammed to the ground and beat instead of simply placing cuffs on him merely sliding his already raised hands behind his back.

Until we get this faction under control, we will continue seeing miscarriages of justice, and law enforcement officers won't gain the trust and respect they should enjoy from the people. The public and the law should operate together as one and that's where the blue will gain the respect and trust it should enjoy from the public.

Law and order in our nation has seen so much improvement, yet so much work remains to be done when certain officers take the law into their own hand and commit crimes against its citizens. When we finally get this misconduct under control, history will have proven that these were crimes committed against humanity.

This problem would be less obvious now if we would have taken care of the problem way back then.

Way back then, accountability should have been enforced and today the problem would have been all but eliminated. Because of corruption, this problem hasn't been addressed and the situation has exploded to our streets where innocent men, women and children are being gunned down and hunted, almost as bad as our old wild wild west.

The problem has also invaded our schools and left our students unprotected when the officer who is supposed to be standing guard at the school, runs and hides when he hears gun shots, instead of going towards the hostility and at least trying to repel an attack.

Way back then, we should have given our officers better training and if we had, then today we wouldn't see our officers gunning down unarmed innocent people or running away from the action, even after they have sworn to uphold, guard and protect these lives. And we would not see our police officers putting their knee into the neck of a suspect until he suffocates to death, or we would not see an unarmed suspect shot in the back seven times.

I believe technology has evolved to a point to where every police officer should wear a body camera. This advancement will improve relations with the police and the public.

I see problems with abuse of these cameras as they're suddenly turned off or failed to operate right as reported by the officer. But to fix this problem for instance, an on-duty officer's camera should never be turned off as long as he or she is on duty. This will answer many questions and keep down confusion. If an officer's camera is turned off during his or her shift, then there should be procedures to go through to keep the public's trust and to ensure that accountability has not been compromised. To turn on or to turn off your recording device should not be a choice of an on-duty police officer. It should always be on. If not, it has been compromised.

Better training would have prevented an overzealous prosecutor from helping railroading an innocent man to prison, but ethics should have also come into play here as well. It's like a domino effect with corruption, all hands are in it to see what they can get out of it personally. And there's an endless supply of money to use because it's all being charged to the public.

With my case, obviously a frame job, however, the state of Missouri has been billed great sums as it wages a war on an unsuspecting and underprivileged proven innocent man by the United States Supreme Court.

The Cape Girardeau Police Department created false witnesses using a system of hypnosis administered by one of its own policemen, creating and falsifying evidence and making a case while breaking the law themselves, showing total disregard for my life, limb or liberty, and no regard for a law it should uphold.

I can only imagine the amount the state of Missouri has been charged in my case alone. For the Missouri Attorney General's office to take this case to Washington, D.C. and present it before the United States Supreme Court twice has to be a staggering number within itself. Yet to date, no accountability has been applied.

It certainly has been an epic battle in my life and for the state to continue to deny me due process is more than painful.

Even though I won my case against the state of Missouri, the state has been allowed to repress my civil rights in a way and manner which has never before been done denying me the equal chance to pursue happiness.

Continuously showing up harassing and disrupting

my life while invading my privacy, with embarrassing and humiliating behavior and conduct. This conduct has had a severe impact on my life and has caused catastrophic change for me.

Whenever I mention accountability, it seems like suddenly I become the target and certain behavior is socially accepted and no one should challenge this illegal conduct. It seems to have even invaded our White House as the President acts more like a bully than a Commander-in-Chief.

You would think that a civil society would demand accountability but when innocent people are still being beat, locked up or even killed irresponsibly, and the guilty being shielded by the law, it's apparent that accountability is not being enforced. How can we as a society keep loving and respecting law enforcement and law enforcement does not love and respect us back?

I believe it would be so easy to stop these abuses, because once the corrupt realizes they're going to be held responsible for their bad behavior, these bad habits will all but stop happening because these people realize they will have to answer for their mischievous acts.

In most cases, good vetting and good information

training and education would weed out any bad recruit during their training and field exercises. However, some officers bond as clicks, groups and there are always plenty mavericks looking to make a name for themselves.

Live body cameras are going to take care of a lot of our accounting problems, but we will need to crack down hard on fraud and misuse of these devices.

When Mom told me to stay out of the cookie jar, I really didn't hear her until I was caught red-handed and Mom slapped my hand as a punishment. But without any repercussions for raiding the jar, the abuse will continue until all the cookies are gone. Will the public continue to allow corruption to consume the cookies until they're all gone?

These illegal acts of contempt will continue in our society until we make the penalty automatic and equally applied across the board.

This level of enforcement will have a deafening effect on any future corruptive behavior, and I believe will eventually eliminate it altogether. But as long as we continue harboring and sheltering corruption, we will continue to see the innocent beat to death, unjustly incarcerated or murdered in the streets.

America is too great of a country to keep looking past these abuses. It's time we hold our leaders accountable for their bad conduct.

I personally have given a lifetime of service towards fighting these crimes and now my work continues through the stroke of my pen as I will always stand up for justice and always stand up for righteousness. I will always stand up for the flag of the United States of America, the greatest nation on this planet. I have proven my loyalty and devotion through my service.

Every time I hear our national anthem being played, I'm almost brought to tears as I remember all the pains involved in us getting to this place and time.

To so many people, the national anthem is merely a song or simple words but when you've seen what I've seen or experienced what I have, the anthem becomes more than mere words. The choice of honoring our flag becomes an issue embedded in the heart and in your life.

To me, that flag represents freedom and justice. It represents all the lives that have been sacrificed in order for us to enjoy all these privileges we enjoy today.

That song and flag mean freedom and commitment. It means all the lives of our martyrs were given up for a cause. For us to let these freedoms be stolen by corrupt acts gives me great pain especially when I view the tombs of a national cemetery or a monument like the Vietnam War Wall or the Martin Luther King Memorial in Washington, D.C.

I see thousands of black Civil War soldiers charging into battleground action not fearing for their lives because they are fighting and forging a new nation and a new way of life.

I see my Uncle Jack charging the beaches of Normandy after our forces had regrouped after Pearl Harbor and now were on the offensive and headed straight towards Berlin. My uncle and his Sherman tank are both a human shield and a sitting target, as the old tank matriculated its way up while blazing the trail in the thick of all the action while paving a way towards change and progress.

And I see my civil case headed back to court possibly even to the United States Supreme Court again, as I continue to expose a gang of outlaws who has corrupted our legal system and has discriminated and abused its networks, for profit and for personal gain.

Corruption is a war in our nation and until we declare war on this beast, we will continue to be pained by the atrocities issued out by these outcasts. Unfortunately, we will see these ills until we make a full declaration of war on them, and it will start when we hold these jokers accountable for their mischievous conduct.

I will personally attest to the fact that the job of a policeman is a hard job. It is a job we volunteer for and so often, it's a job given to a person who has an agenda to serve his or her own ego. But regardless of who occupies the blue, the training to wear the color makes all the difference. When your brother's wife's cousin is given the job without any formal training and is released out on the public, we will see cases where an unarmed man is shot in the back 20 times and the blue reports that he felt like his life was in danger. The problem is exemplified when this excuse is accepted and there is not an ounce of accountability enforced.

It's not a secret that the American police originated as a slave catchers patrol. In case that was a secret, then now the cat is out of the bag; surprised?

Back in the days of the slave catcher, the negro was hunted down like an animal but rarely were they killed because a dead negro wasn't worth anything to his or her captor. But they were beat to near death and treated worse than dogs.

As slavery ended these patrols became more violent towards the negro. The killing of these people, beating, torturing, humiliating, and incarceration became a way of life. Quite frankly, not much has changed in all these years except now, more attention is being focused on the abuses and it largely is due to new technology especially these new recording telephones. And how can we ever forget that a lot of this change is because the negro has penetrated the ranks of law enforcement and has helped to cause this change.

These new devices are now showing the whole wide world what's going on but unfortunately these types of crimes have been orchestrated against the underprivileged now for too many years. It is still hard to watch on the television what's really happening even in modern times.

An abuse committed against an indigent or underprivileged doesn't just affect the abused, it can have adverse effects on a whole family. For example, the abused or killed was the chief bread winner in the family and now the entire family will suffer because the abused can't be replaced and now the whole family will go hungry, lose their home, or in short, their lives have permanently been changed.

When I was seven years old and living as a sharecropper on a cotton plantation, my daddy was forced away from the family by the racists. He fled up north to Michigan to stay with his relatives up there until he regrouped and came back to Mississippi to retrieve his family. Even though daddy had made a promise that he would return, I was always fearful that I would never see him alive again. I was lucky because when daddy appeared unannounced, I ran to him and hugged him hard for as long as I could. I said, "Daddy, I thought I would never see you again." And everywhere he went I went with him, holding his hand. I remember people asking daddy why that boy won't let go of yo hand.

My daddy would tell people how I'd grabbed him and said those words, "He said he thought he'd never see me again," all the way up to his death which happened less than seven years later. But I tried to spend as much of those last seven years with him that I could.

I always try to relate my own personal experiences of the loss of my dad to losses people go through these days. But how do you relate to the things that are still going on today when the racists are still breaking up families and changing lives forever. There just isn't much comparison.

These days, more and more people are coming together to try to make a change, but change will not take place until we get this police issue under control.

It really hurts me so bad to see these abuses happen, now almost on a daily basis. The answer to solving these abuses has been right in front of us and right before our eyes. It's called accountability.

If we don't enforce accountability, then forget about ever fixing the problem and egotistical maniacs will continue invading the ranks of our law enforcement. Racism will continue to thrive in America. What a shame.

From America's earliest days, people have sought to find deeper meaning to human life. Religion, cultural values, and codes of ethics have always influenced social customs, laws and forms of government. It's a shame accountability hasn't played a more forceful role in these developments.

To provide for their security, minorities and the less fortunate have created their own communities and organizations. But when these separate groups or communities have become too prosperous, the racist has raided these areas and destroyed them, and often they commit these abuses in the name of the law. A prime example of this is the raid and total destruction of the black area in Tulsa, Oklahoma, in the early part of the 1900's. Not a single one of those racists ever stood to account for the killings and total annihilation of a productive and thriving black community.

Black people and the black society have been affected by the physical world in which they exist. I believe it's fair to say that our black community has not yet even today recovered from the atrocities committed against them. Without accountability in place, it's fair to say that our communities never will recover. For that matter, they never can recover.

Because we haven't been accepted by the elite groups, we've tried to develop our independence. Independence is essential to freedom, and that freedom is essential to leading a full life. The struggle for rights has been reflected in the struggles for the vote, for economic freedom, for personal liberties and for independence. There are few nations whose history hasn't been marked by a struggle for rights among its people and yet without some form of accountability, these struggles become almost impossible to achieve.

Since creation, people have made scientific discoveries and technological innovations that have changed the world. New discoveries can bring benefits or pose new dangers to the world. I believe it's safe to say that the new telephone cameras have posed a new threat to the abuses of the racist and is the weapon which will bring about some much needed change.

Let us make a declaration of war on the racist, because this war the racist has fought against us has caused immeasurable devastation. Wars have always meant destruction and disruption to some level. In the modern period, wars usually have brought greater devastation than in earlier epics.

The Tulsa destruction, the East St. Louis massacre, and the day of the rope has been genocide and ethnic cleaning of the negro and these are but a few characterizations of wars of the twentieth century. Recovering from such losses is costly, and the desire for revenge or triumph can color the attitudes of an entire generation. Yet the negro has remained loyal, humble and devoted to the cause of justice but without more strict accountability, this position of loyalty will not continue. I don't believe they can continue this devotion especially now that these abuses are currently being shown to the whole world.

A totalitarian system violates human rights in pursuit of power. These systems have been firmly entrenched in America through our police, but change is for sure on the way, thanks to new technology like these cellular phones and a stricter form of accountability that's now transforming our police departments. By definition, the totalitarian state smothers the individuality of its citizens. This system seeks to control political, economic, social, intellectual and cultural areas of life and does so through propaganda and through force.

Apparently it's too much to ask for accountability because to date, it's been tossed to the wind. These guys are not even slapped on the hand before they're released back out on the public.

My personal experience has been that when I push for accountability, I am black-balled and labeled anti-police. What kind of nation are we really if we can't hold our leaders accountable to the public they have sworn to serve and to protect? That should be a high priority and it should be the law. America is become two-faced and in denial of the plain facts. We need to put an end to this abuse of power and it all starts with body cameras and stricter accountability.

Of course ethics should be a high priority for us if we are to bring our law back to being under control. But as long as our legal system allows lawyers to shift favors for convictions, or bribes for jobs, our system will be in dire straits. The innocent and underprivileged will most always be the ones to suffer the heaviest consequence.

Ethics wouldn't have allowed an overzealous prosecutor to proceed forward with only fabricated evidence, if a system of justice was firmly in place and functioning as needed, to combat cases like mine where a victorious prosecutor openly boasts to the media that the conviction was gained with little or no evidence. And I strongly emphasize the no evidence once the judge threw out all the hypnosis mess leaving the prosecuting team nothing to push forward with exception for the integrity of their police department. A department which functioned like this department behaved has a lot to be desired. The time has run out to change it.

An overzealous prosecutor, an underfunded public defender network, and a system of low ethics have created a monster of a problem for our legal system to solve. To date, no one is willing to seriously address the issue because it's too easy to get your hand into the public trusts. A lot of those who are in mostly will take until there's nothing more to take. Behaving like childhood bullies taking more than your share and putting the public at risk.

Poor ethics have invaded our system so heavily that even our president is acting more like a mob boss than a president. When he tries to bully the strongest police officer in the world, he tries to put him in his pocket.

Thank God, some ethics prevailed as the chief American policeman FBI Director Agent James Comey stood up to the president and said no sir, I won't do that, Mr. President. Comey knew that standing up to the president meant that he would lose his job for being disobedient. That's the kind of pride we should all cheer and support and the kind of ethics we should demand from those we've entrusted to carry the badge, seal and protection of the total weight, power and support of the United States of America.

It's what all the hoopla is about with everyone wanting and trying to get to America.

They come with visions of justice and with ideas

that will shape and change the world.

They come in chains and against their will but with hopes of freedom and dreams that will empower and build a new nation.

They come as immigrants and as peasants and gypsies looking for a new way of life, having heard of a new place where freedom rang and justice is for all.

They come as hobos with only the clothes on their backs.

And they come as refugees to show their families and loved ones a new place and a new beginning, as the atrocities of open violence have invaded their homeland. America gives them hope, like a shining beacon to a lost ship America is calling to them. Come! Bring me your tired and hungry. At least, that was once the call.

We've all gathered here hoping for peace and freedom but the resistance to the struggle has caused so much unnecessary suffering that corruption has invaded our key positions of society. They continue to harbor an element of hate and discrimination well embedded and alive and well in our nation.

But there's a solution to this madness. There's only one way to get this beast under control. That's accountability.

You really can't say that we've ever had this beast under control because it's taken the blood of our martyrs, the whip, the branding iron, the rope of the vultures, and the building of a system of justice, to get us to this point and to this place and time.

Oh no, it hasn't been easy forging and chartering a new system of fairness, but accountability is what has smoked the beast out of his darkness. It's what will eventually bring us equality and justice for all.

I don't think that's asking for too much from those we've entrusted to lead or wear the blue, to be accountable. They've already shown a willingness to accept responsibility, so when they pin on the badge or take an oath, it becomes an obligation to account for one's action and whether police, public officers or otherwise.

Some have perverted the system by maybe accepting responsibility for their actions, but they fail to disclose the results in a timely or transparent manner. This type of behavior is what shields the corrupt and is a practice that has no life in a system where accountability is enforced.

Let's try to solve this problem by creating a culture

of accountability. In a short period, we will see this problem of corruption all but take care of itself.

Simply thinking about goals won't yield very many results. The one critical component of bringing a desired goal to fruition is accountability.

When we apply accountability, this will patrol as its own checks and balances system overlapping the public, the position and purpose of fairness. It will create a culture of justice long overdue and well deserved.

I believe America will continue leading the way in human justice as we realize the important of accountability. With the assistance of the body camera, we will see these abuses all but fade away.

The American police has been a very intricate part in all the progress we've made in this nation. It will be the police who brings some healing to a nation in much pain. This healing has already started as we start putting a system of accountability in place.

Chapter 9

Bonded

Like the brush of the artist, some creations can't be revealed until the painting is completed. In my life for instance, the total picture shows a corrupt police department being shield by the courts. Yet it's the court system that ultimately unravel the abuses caused by the gang of criminals perpetrating as a police department.

It's almost too unbelievable to conceive how the United States Supreme Court can free a man from prison because the cops broke the law in convicting him by using fabricated evidence. Then, the corrupt cops come back to haunt him 31 years later concerning the 31-year-old case and this is not considered harassment.

Except for a letter I'd write here and there, or being triggered by an event on television, it had been 31 years and I'd moved on past the prison railroading and was making really good with my life in spite of the ball and chain I carried. I had taken over a production department at a stable medium size company. My boss and plant manager, who was also the owner's son-in-law, was more than happy to let me run the show since it took a lot of pressure off of him. This relief of workload off the boss allowed him to concentrate on other things and he eventually went on to run the whole company.

Within five years, I had almost total control over production now running the whole company through the production of my department.

The boss' son-in-law moved on into the front office and put another plant manager in charge. The new plant manager was only a puppet to me, because he had to come to me for production information.

Things were really going well for me and over 30 years had passed since I'd been freed from prison. I was making good money.

Out of nowhere, here came the Cape Girardeau

Police Department, 125 miles away with a warrant for my arrest saying that it was a mistake that I was let out of prison. "You only got out on a technicality," they yelled.

That day was December 14, 2011, and it was the last day I worked for a company that had been kept afloat because of my skills, knowledge of production, and hard work. Within one year of my departure, there was a noticeable difference in production, quality, and number of descending orders. With the loss of my productivity, the company lost most of its contracts. The company had won so many bids on jobs because of my hard work, but now barely made it once I was gone. It stayed afloat depending on the state contract job it managed to get every now and then. Within five years, a thriving commercial paper production company was tattered and in ruins. It dissolved at the end of the fifth year after I left.

I knew my company would decimate without my work around there once I was gone. The last ten years had only been made possible because I commandeered a mismanaged company and kept it afloat with skills that I can still boast about because the almost 20 years I walked the floor of that factory in St. Louis,

Missouri, made me a legend in the factory and in the cutting industry. I would often hand cut over one million envelopes a day.

When other company executives visited our company, often my production had a strong influence on their visit. Of the ten different machines in my department, I learned the personality and operation of each of these machines and most of the machines were old machines. I mean very very old. I was the only one in the company who had those skills.

That repoire with administration got me into a golf tournament that I could not have entered without those ties. Representing my company, I won that golf tournament. Even though it was a four-man scramble, 75% of my shots were used and my shot making abilities often kept the team in line to win.

I mean, things were really going well for me until the Cape Girardeau Police Department showed up at my factory, threatening, harassing and changing my life. Two of the Cape Girardeau policemen got up early at 3:00-4:00am, and drove over 125 miles one way to come barge in on me at my place of employment I had been at for the last almost 20 years.

About 9:30am, the plant manager came to my

department and asked me to come to the office where these two Cape cops and three Brentwood cops ushered me into a side office and hit me with this frivolous warrant.

After everything I'd already gone through, I thought they were going to lock me up again because they kept saying I had only gotten out on a technicality. They had already railroaded me once before. I was concerned.

I suddenly became confused and without answers. Didn't the United States Supreme Court settle the issue decades ago? Can they come back and put me in jail over these charges again?

Modern technology has replaced the ball and chain with an ankle bracelet. I suddenly felt tied and bounded up again. Even though I'd been freed from prison, the Cape Girardeau Police Department tracked and harassed me like I'm their criminal to do and use as they see fit. Any time they wanted to arouse me, they feel like they can regardless of the ruling from the United States Supreme Court setting me free. So they stalked me and paid me a visit 31 years later to remind me that they are still there. I suddenly felt like I was permanently tied to them like a ball and chain with very little recourse.

I felt like they tracked me like I was wearing the

ankle bracelet.

But this bully has really only ignited a fire inside of me for justice and now that the bully has been exposed, it's time for some restitution.

For 40 years I've patiently waited on the day that the bully police department is held accountable. This department has denied the absolute facts even after being handed the ruling from the United States Supreme Court. This department refuses to follow the court's ruling.

I can't help wondering how many millions of dollars have been already charged to the public to punish me and these state lawyers spent countless days in Washington, D.C., arguing their frivolous case to the nine Supreme Court judges who saw through their lies, and set me free. Those little country cops in Cape came up with a clever game to entrap an innocent man, conceal and suppress the truth, and railroad a man to prison. This was a cold calculated and brazen abuse of the law. And to do it so convincingly while horribly misusing the law is the work of hate exercised to its absolute fullest degree.

My athletic abilities always made me ready to take on any challenge, but when the police is the bully, they're being funded and often supported by the public. How can an indigent and innocent man take on or challenge such authority?

It has been mostly true grit and pure determination that I've been able to resist this powerful beast. The creation of the internet has been instrumental in arming me with knowledge and techniques, to help me better cope with my foes. It has given me much hope and promise that my voice too can be heard.

Having all of your pleas for justice blocked by power plays can be quite frustrating, but the pursuit of justice gives me strength and motivation. It is this force that now pushes this pen and encourages the spirit towards greater achievements.

But 40 years has given me much evidence as to what happened in my life as these bumbling crooks left plenty of evidence to collect and to follow. In their powerful positions, they felt like who cares, even if he is found innocent at a later date, he will have already served time. And chances are good that he may never even make it out of prison. The corrupt has no one to answer to believing that he has gotten away with the bad behavior.

Yogi said, "It ain't over til its over." Some say it

ain't over until the fat lady sings. And it ain't over in fact the fat lady hasn't even starting warming up her voice. But when the fat lady does sing, like the walls of Jericho, a lot of powerful things are going to come tumbling down.

Because of the criminal activities of the Cape Girardeau Police Department, I have been permanently bonded to this case. Anything and everything I do will always bring this case front and center and leave me explaining to others my involvement in this case or lack thereof.

If I apply for any job, the first thing that comes up, if I'm lucky enough to get an interview, is my involvement in this case that these crooks forced on me.

Nothing I do can shake this image or change how I'm looked at because this ordeal follows me everywhere. It always manages to find its way into the conversation.

One of the key reasons I started writing my books is because I wanted people to understand the whole story and not be left in the dark about what happened to me.

Often I would meet new people. Some wanted to know who you were and what have you done. Often I found myself trying to explain to them but in the end I realized that I had left out some key elements that would leave my new acquaintance in question or leave a serious flaw in my character. This was often very embarrassing to me and would sometimes leave me feeling lesser of myself or feeling empty inside. That's what really pushed me to write. Also, writing was an avenue that helped me release some of the pressure I carried inside of me.

But being securely bonded to this case hasn't been easy. Sometimes, the load is still heavy to carry.

There are some people who will never let you live down what has happened to you. It's those people that make me realize that I'm permanently bonded, shackled and chained to this case forever.

Every time I applied for a job, I realized that I am bonded to this case. Whenever I see something about the Cape Girardeau Police Department, Judge Stephen Limbaugh jr. or John Ashcroft, I'm reminded that I will always be bonded shackled and chained to this case forever.

A lot of people who know me have been left in shock that I've had to live my life carrying this ball and chain. My life before I was railroaded was a life of service as a law abiding citizen and it still is. It's amazing that this bunch has successfully managed to bond me to such a case and has managed to avoid being held accountable, even after having been admonished and defeated by the highest court in the land. I have managed to keep my head held up high even as I still carry the ball and chain I carry. One day I hope to break this bondage and free myself from the shackle and chains that have held and bonded me for over 40 years now.

After 40 years I am still fighting this bondage. I still actively seek to hold my captors responsible in a civil action, but all my attempts are still being blocked. My actions in court are still being held back, but my actions filed is educating me and keeping my hopes alive that someday I will be free of the bondage that bounds me. These captors will finally have to let go of my toe.

One of the oldest black men who knew me asked me just before he died, "Hey son, did those people ever let your toe go?" Not yet, I answered, but I'm still working on it.

It was my misfortune that I never got to talk to him again before he died. This old man never doubted me and always found a way to lift up my spirits whenever we were together.

I would often stop by his barber shop where a lot of older black gentlemen would gather. Every time I'd walk into his business, he always had some positive words of encouragement for me.

His favorite line upon my arrival to his business was, "Looky here, that there is Legendary Leon Little", or he would say, "Well here comes the only black state trooper from this part of the state." His business was often very busy and those words always managed to raise the heads of all the gentlemen who were there. Even with all his words of encouragement, we both knew that I had been bonded, shackled and chained to this fictitious case for the rest of my life.

I don't know if it will ever happen, or when or how it will happen, but my hopes and dreams are to be free. I'll never give up on those feelings because I yearn to be free of the bondage, shackle and chains that I've carried for over two thirds of my life.

In a sense I probably should feel lucky to be alive, because the very first day these crooks kidnapped me, Cape Girardeau police officer Bill McHughes rushed me with a choke hold and was pulled off of me by his partner. I knew then that I was in a fight for my life. But I still had strong beliefs in our justice system and I was hoping to free myself in court. When I got to court, I realized these people had fabricated a real good noose and that bondage made me feel like a George Floyd; take your knee off of my neck, "I can't breathe."

I was also reminded of the man my dad had taken me to see who had the racists break into his house and hung him right in front of his family and loved ones who had to stand by helpless as the racists carried on in the name of the law.

Well, the old man is gone now, George Floyd is gone now too, and so is my dear dad, but the feelings of the bondage, shackle and chains are still etched in the reservoir of my mind forever.

Sometimes I feel like I can't breathe, but thank God, I'm still alive and the beast didn't suffocate me to death.

Today some look at me and may want to believe I am living the dream with the beautiful family I have. I have even added to my wonderful family since my release a lovely wife who has given me the beautiful Taylor and my super stud Trevor. But my man Zach was my first creation once I was released from prison, and Mr. Zach has given me beautiful grandchildren Mason and Evie and a lovely daughter-in-law Nikki. My oldest daughter Tara has also enriched my life with two grandchildren Tala and Tristan.

When I see my creations, I often question myself, am I living the dream? When I hear their voices, I ask myself, am I living the dream? But when I see what the systemic racist has done to me, I'm rudely awakened to reality that I'm bonded shackled and chained to this injustice for the rest of my life.

Chapter 10

Who Made Who

INCARCERATING INNOCENT PEOPLE is a very lucrative business especially when you're being shielded from the law, because you are the law. The most powerful fact supporting that statement is the institution of slavery. Up to this point in my case, everyone is charging the public; from the police department to the prosecutor's office, except no money is allotted to the defense of the accused who is indigent. But what is even more appalling is that the accused is being framed and set up.

Most of the time, anyone caught up in this trap will often spend time in prison, but these corrupt officials are making choices involving the lives of innocent men and women, usually ruining these lives forever. Personally, as I walked through my experience, I felt more like I was being persecuted rather than prosecuted. Tomorrow or the next day was my goal as I fought this injustice and tried to stay alive each day.

With evidence of a most suspicious nature, a hot shot prosecutor stirs up the rhetoric, positioning himself as a tough no nonsense prosecutor in an election for a position as a federal judge, using the photograph of a negro and a gorilla to identify a rising star. This prosecuting attorney wins the seat on the federal bench but he keeps his hands on this case and tries to manipulate it whenever possible.

Before Judge Stephen Limbaugh jr. recused himself from this case, he did sign several documents involving the case which I believe was an illegal act. Limbaugh was now worried that this case had resurfaced and he probably hoped that he could put out the fire before it ever got started. What he did was prove his continued involvement and even further illegal acts on his behalf.

When Limbaugh was elected as a federal judge, his

hands should have been free of this case except they were not. He's still allowed to sign papers concerning this case and his influence over the case, I believe, is what has kept a civil suit from going forward.

So far, this phony case made up of fabricated and racially charged evidence has made and put a public defender on the map, and made two prosecuting attorneys, one who is now a federal judge. This case also made an attorney general at state and federal levels, John Ashcroft as Missouri Attorney General and as United States Attorney General.

John Ashcroft inherited this case as Missouri Attorney General and fought it to the United States Supreme Court, where he lost the case. At this point in my case, I don't believe Ashcroft really cared that he pushed forward a case based on an identification of a suspect using a gorilla and an illegal hypnosis. He was too deeply involved in the case. This case had gotten him to the United States Supreme Court which I believe is a dream come true for most lawyers. Ashcroft parlayed my case into a position of highest law official in our nation.

While in Washington, D.C. arguing my case, Ashcroft worked his magic and he was eventually chosen as U.S. Attorney General. But why, he lost his argument to the nine judges and still made his way back to Washington D.C. as U.S. Attorney General.

Ashcroft used my case and worked his way straight into Washington, D.C. as he tossed ethics to the wind and tried to rewrite his own way of justice. Ashcroft is now legendary in America as an overzealous prosecuting attorney. Let us give the credit where credit is due. This fabricated case made all these low ethical men who they are today.

It's obviously not a secret that Ashcroft is an overzealous prosecuting attorney as the only sitting Senator to ever host Saturday Night Live made Ashcroft his platform and comedically roasted the man.

As Senator John McCain roasted Ashcroft on Saturday Night Live, I felt a double emotion as I was hurt having been the brunt of Ashcroft's overzealous works. I was humored as Mr. McCain brought to light the works of a hardened man and out of control jurist. It truly is amazing that this lawyer was chosen as Attorney General. Hopefully all of his work wasn't contaminated like my case was, but having gone through this ordeal, I have to question a lot of his work.

Ashcroft made me the scorn of public disgrace while I was being overpowered with inadequate legal counsel and paraded around the state in chains. He pushed forward with fabricated evidence and showed no regard for life, limb or fairness.

With my victory in the United States Supreme Court, you may have thought things are good from there, except pawns have been well positioned and a system has been compromised to keep this innocent man repressed. All of these prosecutors have formed a tag team and now they are all in it together, sticking and staying together showing extreme bias and complicity. This ordeal was hard to deal with then and it continued to be a hard pill to swallow.

An overwhelming mountain of evidence is too monumental to overlook as this case was thought to have been covered up well. Like a fine wine, time has matured the ingredients of evidence and has exposed a super case that has only gotten stronger from trial court to the Supreme Court. Now this case belongs in the civil court where an attempt at reparations could help comfort a loyal, devoted and confused American soldier.

And let's make no mistake about this ordeal. I

am the loyal, devoted and faithful soldier out of this bunch. My service has been voluntary and true, not stolen and on the back of an innocent man.

For profit and gain, Ashcroft becomes U.S. Attorney General for his part in railroading Leon. Stephen Limbaugh jr. becomes a federal judge for his role in this railroading job as the initial prosecuting attorney who stirs up the controversy and hands the case off to the new prosecutor, Larry Ferrell, who too makes millions for himself.

Using fake evidence, these guys manipulate the court system, deceive a jury, and use our justice system to enrich their lives by falsely creating cases and changing lives forever, as they charge the heck out of the public.

When these jokers created this case against me, they not only made work for themselves, they kept the money flowing to others. This was very expensive work these crooks charged to the public. Not even to account for how innocent lives are changed forever.

Ashcroft traveled to Washington, D.C. several times arguing this case to the Supreme Court. I'm sure he stayed at the most expensive hotel in town as he dined on steak and potatoes. He probably used room service often, cowardly hiding in his hotel suite and for good reason, the acts he committed against me are the acts of cowards and racist men.

To bring a case to trial is an exercise of quite some expense and for the prosecuting attorney, there's an endless supply of funds. You know the public trust has deep pockets.

To counsel or represent the case through every phase of the appeal process really pushed the bill over the limit, but for the prosecuting attorney there was no limit. All limitations were sorely carried by the accused, who less add, was innocent and indigent.

But I still managed to fight these jokers, even from behind bars, all the way to the Supreme Court where I defeated the beast and was ordered to be releasd from custody.

So who made who here? That's a question that can be answered when you examine the facts involved in this case. Since all of the evidence in this case was racially charged and fabricated, it is obvious that Stephen Limbaugh jr. and the Cape Girardeau Police Department made the case but what's even more apparent is that I made these officials who they are today.

I take no pride in making these racist clowns who

they are today. These racist clowns have taken great pride in racist behavior, their manipulation of the justice system, and of their skills at keeping their knee on the neck of an innocent man.

George Floyd made the phrase popular, "I can't breathe," and it's so unfortunate that the beast kept his knee on the neck of Mr. Floyd until all the breath was removed from his body.

I have managed to keep breathing even though it's been very difficult at times. Frankly, there were even times where I really didn't care whether I breathed or not.

I believe my case has been scripted of the spirit and has had life breathed into it to help bring about change to a justice system gone astray. I am of the belief that God works in mysterious ways. I believe life has been breathed into this case and now the racist men involved in this case have a new concern and a new worry that keep them from sleeping at night.

Who made who? Let's see: Before me you guys were low level officials going nowhere. Me on the other hand was already a former United States Marine honorably discharged, and the eighth black state rod from my state and only 21 years old and now. . . . I'm a writer. So put another notch in your belt, fellas, because you can now take credit for making me a writer as well and this pencil is aimed directly at you.

Don't get too relaxed because I plan to turn the heat up a lot more. I can see you racists squirming about and hollering that it's getting hot in here. For me, I'd like you to yell those words from behind bars because what you fellas did to me was nothing short of criminal. The whole lot of you should spend time in jail.

I believe that you guys have put so many innocent men and women in jail, some to their deaths. What's good for the goose is good for the gander. But it will be our justice system that I hope will eventually take care of you.

You know, there's enough criminal activity happening out there that our police and law officials don't need to be making up cases on people and railroading innocent men and women to jail. But in my case, these racists deliberately stalked a rising negro and deliberately stole all of his hard work and service. You should be ashamed of yourselves but I'm sure you have very little, if any, guilt because all your lives, you've roamed around like America owes you something, and that you can use it anyway you see fit. This is ours, and, no, you don't have the right to use the justice system for your personal, political profit and gain. If you believe that this system belongs to you, then think again, because a new movement has been started. We are in the process of taking our justice system back away from the racist and placing it back firmly into the hands of its rightful owners, the American people.

You've had plenty of time to pervert our system in your favor. For years, it has made you and your loved ones tons and tons of revenue. But be prepared to loosen your grip and even be prepared to let go altogether because this is not yours. Quite contrary to what you've preached and taught all of your lives, this belongs to the people. Let's see, how does our constitution begin, We the People. That doen't mean we the racist or corrupt so let go. Contrary to how you have operate our system all your lives, I'm sure that you too will be treated equally and will finally embrace the phases, We the People, equal protection and equal justice for all.

Chapter 11

Too Wrong For Too Long

Many folks realize that systemic racism is a real issue in our country and for those who don't, chances are, they're part of the problem itself.

It has been over 400 years of fighting for freedom and equality and the history that was taught to us in our schools often left out or misrepresented the struggle and the long people's fight for equality.

I believe more recognition should be directed to the over 400 years of struggling and that Americans should commemorate the fierce battle and anniversaries of enslaved Africans first arriving in Jamestown,

Virginia, in 1619. The system after those defining moments codified inequality in law and customs.

Addressing this legacy of injustice is intimately connected to the struggle for rights of all oppressed people. We've all got to come together as a coalition of organizations and individuals and to dedicate ourselves to dismantling structural inequality. This will evitably help us build a strong and healthier country and communities.

I strongly believe that a national observance of the lasting impact of slavery on the American society and government is key to healing and building a more just future. Oppression has truly deprived us of having a more free society. Building coalitions will challenge inequality and through coalitions we can create and build a more equitable society.

I stand by the declaration that "Nobody's free until everybody's free" and "Injustice anywhere is a threat to justice everywhere. We are caught in an inescapable network of mutuality, tied in a single garment of destiny."

The ghost of slavery and the curse of racism still threaten us over 400 years later because the colonizers and founding fathers sowed seeds of strife into the soil of liberty. Our inability to confront and to overcome this wicked legacy helped manifest the elite and resurgent of white nationalism that, if underestimated, could trigger the first sectional crisis in our nation since the American Civil War.

Our history from colonialism to present is marked with events and debates that underscore the nature of slavery and racism in the American enterprise. The Compromise of 1820, for example, admitted Missouri into the Union as a slave state and Maine as a free state, maintaining the political balance between North and South, led to a profound reckoning.

In a letter to John Holmes, the inaugural United States senator from Maine, Thomas Jefferson prophesied ominously: "We have the wolf by the ear, and we can neither hold him nor safely let him go. Justice is in one scale and self-preservation in the other."

Jefferson's wolf was an allegory of the deadly dimensions of slavery and racism. The wolf symbolized the republic's propensity for fratricide: the high point of which culminated in the Civil War and its aftermath. Yet, more than 150 years after that war, our grip on the wolf of white supremacy remains weak, and the wolf continues to be our nation's most enduring existential threat.

The ways of the wolf predate the founding of this republic. In the 1600's, fluid settler colonial societies composed of unfree African and European labor, gradually hardened into a regime of brutal racial slavery. From denying Africans the right to bear arms to restricting their movements, colonial authorities did everything in their power to divide disenfranchised Africans and Europeans. In fact, what we now call white privilege is largely the outcome of similar structural schemes wealthy settlers implemented to elevate poor whites over blacks. This policy safeguarded elites from interracial revolution, especially after Bacon's Rebellion in 1676, when disenfranchised whites and blacks took up arms together.

For this reason, the late Edmund Morgan, the authority on the history of the colonial era and early republic, wrote, "The rights of Englishmen were preserved by destroying the rights of Africans." So engrained is white supremacy and black repression, for example, that Chief Justice Roger Taney concluded in 1857 that a black person "had no right which the white man was bound to respect."

The nearly unchoked campaigns of racial terrorism that former Confederate soldiers inflicted on

African Americans during Reconstruction, including disenfranchisement and the overthrow of democratically elected African American statesmen in the post- Reconstruction years and the emergence of the "separate but equal" Jim Crow doctrine in 1896, among many other crimes, reaffirm Morgan's and Taney's assertions.

Jim Crow and racial terrorism continued unabated even up until now. But civil rights legislation in the 1950's and 1960's begin to slowly correct the effects of centuries of brutality and injustice against the enslaved and their descendants: White suburbanites doubled down on segregation and white politicans on the left and right have shown championed punitive measures that sparked mass incarceration. Black subjugation has been integral to white self-determination and white liberation.

No wonder legions of white voters across this country yearn for racial revanchism, unable to recognize the merits of interracial cooperation, even along class lines. From birth, the United States racial order conditions most white citizens that true freedom for them necessitate signs of despair for black citizens.

Morgan's "American paradox" thesis, which

stipulated that racial slavery and the subordination of blacks allowed democratic liberalism to flourish for the benefit of rich and poor whites, remain one of the incontrovertible truths about United States history.

Simply put, poor whites are willing to accept exploitation by white elites, as long as poor whites think they are better positioned in the pecking order than African Americans, the nation's perennial sacrificial lamb. Whenever African American self-assertion disrupted the system of racial and economic caste, a swift backlash occurred. Anti-lynching activist Ida B. Wells, as a result, attributed many lynching to white anxiety over black economic progress.

Coinciding with the elite and resurgent white nationalism, the 400th anniversary of slavery in the United States has inspired renewed scrutiny of the curse of the color caste on our collective consciousness. Indeed, a new "Era of the wolf" is upon us. The widening wealth and health gaps between African Americans and whites, hyper-criminalization and mass incarceration of African Americans, the meaning and future of affirmative action, and efforts to save Confederate flags and memorials are but a few contentious issues that will trigger further conflict.

One cannot say categorically the extent to which these events will galvanize working class African Americans, the intended but forgotten beneficiaries of the civil rights movements. No group in United States history has withstood more hardship with fewer resources, overcoming greater odds to assert their humanity than the enslaved and their descendants. The Rev. Martin L. King Jr. described the log of many as a "triple ghetto" of race, poverty and human misery. Dr. Martin Luther King, however, indicated something of seismic proportions is afoot.

The subject of reparation for slavery, Jim Crow and other injustices have resurfaced organically and forcefully among African Americans. In the lead up to 2020, some Democratic presidential hopefuls, seeking to harness or to co-opt rising frustration among African Americans, were openly discussing the possibility of reparations, once a fringe demand.

Before the Black Lives Matter movement erupted, this grass-rooted push for reparations and the need to recognize the unique history and experience of descendants of the enslaved was the biggest black-led social movement in over 50 years.

In the allegory of the wolf, Jefferson deliberately

overlooked a vital point: Justice is the key to United States self preservation. The two are mutually reinforcing, not exclusive. After over 400 years of racial slavery, racial terrorism and racial caste, the nation must reckon with the debt (in whatever form) owed to African Americans. Not even immigrants – new and old, black and non-black – are exempt from this impending national reckoning. We all have benefitted enormously from the sweat and blood of the enslaved and their descendants who mostly built this nation, and whose agitation for full citizenship gave everyone additional rights and privileged.

The longer racial justice is delayed for African Americans, and the longer it takes to confront the tragic history of elites and politicians who pit ordinary whites against blacks, the sooner the nation will devour itself. Only once the wolf of racial and economic caste is destroyed can we truly secure justice and self-preservation in the United States of America.

So many people don't even realize that the first African Americans arrived into what would become the United States of America, a full year before the Mayflower ever landed here. So try to understand that this isn't your country that you boast about with these racist ideas. This is all of our country.

Historians, elected political figures and some community leaders would prefer to sort of imagine the United States as a kind of mythic, Anglo-Saxon place. They'd like to believe that in this country, American means white and that everybody else has to hyphenate. I believe that that couldn't be further from the truth.

Many Americans' introduction to United States history is the arrival of the passengers on the Mayflower, but even before that, 20 enslaved Africans were already here against their will and already working on the legacy which would become the United States of America.

Four hundred years on, the captives' arrival has informed nearly every major moment in American history, even if that history has been framed around anyone but Africans and African Americans.

After the first captives were forced to Virginia's shores, the majority of the country remained white and relied mainly on the labor of others rather than themselves. But real soon, the transatlantic slave trade made its impact on the American colonies.

The first anti-miscegenation statue – prohibiting marriage between races – was written into law in Maryland in 1661, not much after enslaved people were brought to the colonies. By the 1960's, 21 states, most of them in the south, still had those laws in place. Alabama was the last state to repeal the ban on interracial marriage, in the year 2000.

The Declaration of Independence, which embraced in its first line "that all men are created equal, that they are endowed by their creator with certain unalienable rights", did not extend that right to slaves, Africans or African Americans, with the final version scrapping a reference to the denunciation of slavery. Thomas Jefferson, a slave owner himself, penned those lines rejecting slavery; he removed the reference after receiving criticism from a number of delegates who themselves enslaved black people. This could represent "the fabric of the American political economy" ever since, many historians have said.

Slavery flourished in the tobacco fields and eventually spread to rice plantations further south and on to the cotton plantations and beyond.

The British operated slave trade across the Atlantic was one of the biggest businesses of the 18th century.

Approximately ten million African slaves were brought into the American colonies before the slave trade – not slavery – was banned by Congress in 1808.

By 1860, the United States recorded 13% of the population as Africans and African American slaves.

Eight of the first 12 United States presidents were slave owners. Proponents of Slavery supported the efforts of groups like the American Colonization Society, who "sent back" tens of thousands of free black people – most of them American born – to Liberia in the 19th century to prevent disruption caused by free descendants of slaves.

According to Abraham Lincoln, the Civil War was fought to keep America whole, and not for the abolition of slavery – at least initially. Southern states said they wanted to secede to protect states' rights, but they were fighting to keep people enslaved. Lincoln took on the fight for the freedom of slaves, because he was worried the British would support the South in its self-declared self-determination and recognize the south as a separate entity. If Lincoln had made the war about ending slavery, it would have looked bad for the South's fight and the British supporting its cause. Lincoln's death was probably the first casualty of a long civil rights movement that is for sure not yet over.

Many argue that Reconstruction laid the foundation for "the organization of new segregated institutions, white supremacist ideologies, legal rationalizations, extra legal violence and everyday racial terror" – further widening the racial divide among blacks and whites. Others have pointed out that the end of the war left black Americans free but their status "undetermined", with the passing of "codes" to prevent black people from being truly free.

Under the 14th amendment, African American men were granted the right to vote and they were also extended birthright citizenship: and extended to descendants of freed black slaves and immigrants up and to present day.

When the recession of the late 19th century hit the United States, knight riders went out in the dark, burning the homes of African Americans who had bought their own land. These raiders rode up to Washington to demand change as southern white Democrats rolled back many of the limited freedoms from Reconstruction just a couple decades before.

The Jim Crow era of segregation forbade African

Americans from drinking of the same water fountains, eating at the same restaurants, or attending the same schools as white Americans – all lasting until, and sometimes well past, the 1960's.

As African Americans were short of jobs and opportunities during Jim Crow, and as more jobs became available in the north and Midwest, millions of African Americans migrated after World War I. Still, even hundreds of miles away from southern segregation, these migrating Americans were met by "Sundown Towns", where black people were not welcomed after sunset or dark and by restrictions on where they could live in cities.

Oregon's constitution removed its exclusionary clause, prohibiting black people to enter the state in 1926.

In the lead-up to the end of Jim Crow and the civil rights era, the fight continued. For example, in 1948 did the United States military desegregate but it was by executive order.

In 1954, in the *Brown v. Board of Education* ruling, the Supreme Court ruled that segregation was unconstitutional and schools would have to integrate. Civil rights leaders led anti-segregation marches across the country in the 1960's. In 1964, Lyndon B. Johnson signed the Civil Rights Act into law. Bussing African American children to white schools in white neighborhoods was deemed constitutional.

Slavery was gone, but Jim Crow was alive. "Almost all southern African Americans were shut out of the ballot box and the political power it could yield," wrote Edward E. Baptist in *The Half Has Never Been Told: Slavery and the Making of American Capitalism*. The Voting Rights Act of 1965 attempted to correct this, prohibiting racial discrimination in voting and placing restrictions on a number of southern states if they tried to change voting rights laws. Those restrictions were recently overturned in a 2013 Supreme Court ruling.

Voter suppression, another legacy of slavery and its aftermath, is also becoming a more visible issue. Aggressive attempts by mostly ex-Confederate states to limit the vote for poorer communities of color has become more pronounced since the gutting of the Voting Rights Act in 2013.

This country is at a crossroad and is reckoning with centuries of racial injustices.

African American men have been used and abused.

There's no wonder that black men like myself have personal tragic stories to tell and that African Americans continue to suffer at the hand of racists and are bonded, shackled and chained by systemic racism in this country.

Chapter 12

~~~

MY LIFE MATTERS

WITH ALL THE hoopla these days about this life being more important or more valuable than that life, it's hard to focus on how my life, or anyone else's life for that matter is more special than another. I believe that in the eyes of God, everyone's life is precious and each individuals has been created to achieve its own special goal. Everyone is on his or her own mission while on his or her way to heaven.

Personally, a lot of my life has been wasted on listening to an elite group including racists, telling me how I've been cursed, or being repressed economically and/or being denied certain advantages because of the color of my skin.

These repressors have used social and economic pressure, religious and political pressure and they've even passed law and bonded together as groups to apply these pressures on the underprivileged especially the colored races.

Somehow, even with all these repressions, we the underprivileged have found a way to survive. In a lot of cases, we've even been able to thrive under this heavy weight.

Early on, we had to band together as we put all our hope and faith in the Lord for guidance and survival, but modern times have given us new avenues to lead us up and out of the darkness. The biggest and most powerful these days has been to open and peaceful protest these abuses. Out of these protests has sprang a very powerful movement called "Black Lives Matter".

I believe that to say All Lives Matter misses the big picture. That saying, All Lives Matter communicates to black people that their lives do not matter.

The killings of George Floyd, Breonna Taylor, and so many others have not only served to reignite the "Black Lives Matter" movement, but also the furor at its most common rebuttal: "All Lives Matter". The back and forth has been going on for years and when the quote, "elite or privileged", are pressed to say that "Black Lives Matter", these elite or privileged will often echo those famous words, "All Lives Matter".

While some will say All Lives Matter to provoke conflict, others see it as a harmless or as a inclusive remark. But that's not the way most black people experience it.

"My life matters," and if you say, "No, all lives matter," I would say I believe that you believe all lives matter. Because I live the life that I live, I am certain that in this country, all lives don't matter. I know that for a fact, based on the numbers, my life has not mattered; that black women's lives definitely haven't mattered, that black trans people's lives haven't mattered; that black gay people's lives haven't mattered; that immigrants' lives don't matter; that Muslims' lives don't matter. The lives of the indigenous people of this country have never mattered. We could go on and on and on. So when we say, "all lives", are we talking about white lives? Then, if that is so, then let's just say that because it's coded language.

Saying that "Black Lives Matter" does not mean

that "Black Lives Matter" more; it simply means that "Black Lives Matter", as well. A lot of the confusion could very well stem from a fundamental misunderstanding of that. Maybe some people are committed to misunderstanding what we're trying to say when we say that "Black Lives Matter".

No one is saying that your life doesn't matter, when we say that "Black Lives Matter". What we're saying is that all lives can't matter until "Black Lives Matter".

Before the "Black Lives Matter" movement, no one was saying all lives matter because no one felt a need to position themselves that way.

As for when I use the phrase "Black Lives Matter", I would like to be seen in my own unique experience in this world and for to be actually seen and to be valued as a human being.

I am so proud of the "Black Lives Matter" movement because it has allowed me to realize that Hey! My life does matter too.

The "Black Lives Matter" movement builds power to bring justice, healing and freedom to black people all across the globe. The movement was organized to build power and to intervene when violence was inflicted on black communities by the state and vigilantes. The movement has grown and is committed to struggling together and to imagining and creating a world free of anti-Blackness, where every Black person has the social, economic and political power to thrive.

"Black Lives Matter" began as a call to action in response to state sanctioned violence and anti-Black racism. The intention from the very beginning was to connect Black people from all over the world who have a shared desire for justice and to act together in their communities. The impetus for that commitment was and still is the rampant and deliberate violence inflicted on black people by the state, hate groups and/or vigilantes.

"Black Lives Matter" movements took to the streets in search of justice for all of those who have been torn apart by state sanctioned violence and anti-Black racism. The movement has forever changed and the infrastructure has been built for a global network which has become a powerful and political home for many.

Organization of the movement has helped oust anti-Black politicians and has helped win critical legislation to benefit Black lives. It also has changed the terms of the debate on Blackness all around the world.

Through movement and relationship building, "Black Lives Matter" has helped catalyze other movements and has shifted culture with an eye towards the dangerous impacts of anti-Blackness.

The "Black Lives Matter" movement is as powerful as it is because of its membership, its partnerships, and its supporters, its staff and because of me and of you, its people. The continued commitment is the liberation for all Black people and means that the movement is continuing the work of our ancestors and fighting for our freedom because it is now our duty and it is our turn to carry the torch as we march towards equal justice. A march that was started by these unjust acts and now carried on by all those who seek liberty and justice for all.

The movement is committed to healing ourselves and each other and to co-creating alongside our comrades, allies and family, a culture where each person feels seen, heard and supported.

The movement work for freedom and justice for Black people and by extension, for all people.

The movement is unapologetically Black in its positioning. In affirming that "Black Lives Matter", we need not qualify the position to love and desire freedom and justice for ourselves. It is a prerequisite for wanting the same for others.

The movement is part of the global Black family and is aware of the different ways black people are impacted or privileged as Black people who exist in all different parts of the world, and is guided by the fact that all Black Lives Matter regardless of actual or perceived sexual identity, gender identity, gender expression, economic status, ability, disability, religious beliefs or disbeliefs, immigration status, or location.

The mission is self-reflexive and does the work required to dismantle cisgender privilege and uplift Black trans folk especially Black trans women who continue to be disproportionately impacted by trans-antagonistic violence.

The movement is building a space that affirms Black women and is free from sexism, misogyny and environments in which men are center.

The "Black Lives Matter" movement practices empathy and engages comrades with the intent to learn about and connect with their contexts.

The movement makes family-friendly spaces and enables parents to fully participate with their children as it dismantles the patriarchal practice that requires mothers to work double shifts so that they can mother in private even as they participate in public justice work. And the movement embodies and practices justice, liberation and peace in its enagements with one another.

Thank you to the "Black Lives Matter" movement because it has motivated and empowered me to lift up my head and to hold it high and it's answered so many questions that's baffled me for so very long. Yes, my life does really matter. I fully spport the movement that "Black Lives Matter", has started and pray the movement goes on.

I feel a certain connection to my great-great-grandma who was freed from slavery as an old lady, and my great-grandma who was eight years old when all that took place. I believe these special women felt empowered too once they were freed, but it's taken all these years for a movement to empower and to help lift us all up, my prayer is that this movement continues to get more powerful as it continues the work started by our ancestors.

Personally, I believe that the Black Lives Matter movement has already done more for our race than the NAACP ever could or ever will.

The vicious encounters we have experienced in our struggle are now being brought to the forefront as the movement continues to gain momentum, but the drops of blood that are being spilled by our martyrs are often hard to watch as we're now seeing another episode occur almost daily. As more people say enough is enough, it is because of movements like this one that is slowly bringing a gradual pause to these atrocities. I look for an even greater pause in the violence as the movement keeps getting stronger.

So these days, when I ask myself, does my life really matter, I can find solace and comfort and yes, even encouragement, as movements like "Black Lives Matter" help give my life more purpose and value.

I grew up during Jim Crow, separate but equal, segregation, all of the rhetoric of systemic racism but now I feel good about a real movement and it's the "Black Lives Matter" movement. That's something I can see getting even stronger. It is something I can hang my hat on as I look towards the future.

After everything that I've been put through, I can't help but remember the past and all those martyrs who were left hanging at the tree, those lynched and killed unjustly, and all those who lost their lives in the pursuit of freedom and justice. Your lives matters too and all of your lives will never be forgotten. Rest in peace, dear martyrs, compadres, loves ones and friends, through my pen now I will remember you all and through technology and new movements, we will always honor and respect you. And today and right now, I say that hell yes, your life mattered too. And to you, I owe the deepest of gratitude for all that you did for all of us.

Grandmothers Maggie and Becky were freed from slavery but I'm almost positive that they never dreamed that it would take this long period of time for a serious movement to come along that would bring us real change and to call the racist to account for its corrupt behavior. Well, grandmommas, we got us a real ambassador of progress and change now, and it's in the form of this movement.

I'm so glad that we've finally said enough is enough. We are now more determined to seek equal justice and fairness that I believe will eventually make our planet a better place to live.

This movement got its start as black people came together and said enough is enough after George Zimmerman was acquitted for the murder of Trayvon

Martin. Today, the movement has a global network and high impact on society.

The "Black Lives Matter" project is now a member-led global network of more than 40 chapters. The members organize and build local power to intervene in violence on Black communities by state and vigilantes.

Black Lives Matter is an ideological and political intervention in a world where Black lives are systematically and intentionally targeted for demise.

Black Lives Matter is an affirmation of Black folks' humanity, our contributions to this society, and to our resilience in the face of deadly oppression.

When Mike Brown was murdered in Ferguson, Missouri, the group really sprang into action in support of the brave and courageous community of Ferguson and St. Louis as they were being brutalized by law enforcement, criticized by media, tear-gassed and pepper-sprayed night after night.

The Black Lives Matter movement recognized and understood that Ferguson, Missouri, was not an averration, but in fact, a clear point of reference for what was happening to Black communities across America.

It is very clear that Black people need to continue

organizing and building Black power across the country. People are hungry to galvanize their communities to end state sanctioned violence against Black people, the way Ferguson organizers and allies were doing. The goal of Black Lives Matter is to support the development of new Black leaders as well as to create a network where Black people feel empowered to determine their destinies in their communities and to take greater control of their own lives.

The Black Lives Matter Global Network would not be recognized worldwide if it weren't for the folks in St. Louis and Ferguson who put their bodies on the line day in and day out, and who continue to show up for Black lives.

After the police shot Jacob Blake in the back seven times, the Black Lives Matter movement experienced historic solidarity. The movement has garnered support on a global proportion and has forced and pushed for police accountability. We are now seeing police in America having to answer for their mischievous behavior. This change is refreshing and well overdue as our police in America has acted more like a vigilante group than as a force whose job is to protect and to serve the people, the very ones who pay their salaries.

It's really a shame the way our police and our justice system have treated black people in America. But It's really encouraging to see the support of the people turning out in force to bring an end to these acts. Hopefully, these new voices will bring a change to the systemic racism that has ravaged our nation from its beginning and has already taken the lives of so many innocent Black people in our country and for that matter, all around the world.

The maiming, abuses and violence have to stop and the force being applied by the Black Lives Matter movement is welcomed and long overdue.

We know as black people that the police don't keep us safe. As long as we continue to pump money into our corrupt criminal justice system at the expense of housing and health to assist the poor and underprivileged, we fail to invest more into helping to develop the indigent and the neglected, we will never be truly safe.

Black global networks have liberated and have traumatized the global community and so many others around the world to take to the streets in peaceful protests.

Black Lives Matter is a peaceful protest and does

not condone violence but often it has been accused of being a violent movement. The violence you might see on television is not a part of the Black Lives Matter movement. Regardless of others intent to try to characterize it as a violent protest, this attempt has failed and the Black Lives Matter movement continues to grow and to thrive.

Black Lives Matter is a target of disinformation and has even been targeted by powerful political leaders including the president of the United States himself. Regardless of this disinformation , the movement thrives. I believe it has brought certain individuals and groups in alignment to do the right thing, make our police accountable and our justice system more just and more equal for all.

There is a lot of work to do but this movement has dove off into the piles of abuse and violence with a force that's never before been seen on this planet. Now that it has, a lot of people are concerned and by right they should be because these atrocities have been going on for way too long.

Black Lives Matter is a decentralized political and social movement advocating for non-violent civil disobedience in protest against incidents of police brutality and all racially motivated violence against black people.

Black Lives Matter is exactly what we need in American to help the black folks deal with the systemic racism. It may be the largest and most powerful movement in the history of the United States of America. People are afraid of this movement and if you've been part of the problem, then you have every right to be afraid. The Black Lives Matter protests have caused as much and even more change in our nation than even the civil rights protests and marches of the 1960's.

That's a powerful statement to make because the civil rights movements of the 1960's forced the U.S. government to move faster to do something about the systemic racism that has ravished our nation from its very beginning. The civil rights movements of the 1960's forced the government to pass laws, amend the constitution and to recognize blacks for the service and contribution to this nation and now, the Black Lives Matter movement is bringing about even more change.

This change is not a gift from our government, it has been soaked in the bloodspill of so many martyrs and soldiers whose front line stands are now showing dividers and proving that these lives indeed was given up for a cause. Yes, your lives mattered.

More pressure will bring about more change and it will allow our martyr in heaven, who lost their lives at the tree, that they too still have a voice in the change that's going on and it's largely being pushed by the Black Lives Matter movement.

When I now dream about the future my kids and grandkids can have in America, I can look to the Black Lives Matter movement directly in the face and say "thank you", thanks every one of you for helping to allow so many of us the chance to live the dream and to live in a more perfect union.

Those are the dreams that our forefathers had for us, both black and white, but one thing hasn't changed. That's our blood which has continued to be red. That is the color of blood that we all share. But too much of our blood has spilled out unjustly and unnecessarily and now the Black Lives Matter movement has moved on to the set like a surgeon to stop the bloodshed and to stop the bleeding and to help heal and recuperate a sick nation in its recovery.

I feel like the Black Lives Matter movement has

forced the racist to at least take his knee off of my neck, but in so many ways I still feel like I'm bonded, shackled and chained, with each and every move I make and every breath I take.

But Black Lives Matter is working on that too.

Chapter 13

Dedicated to My Mom

Nothing in life was more important to me than to have been freed from this mess and rewarded for my troubles, while my mother was still alive. But that didn't happen as mother passed away in 2017 and my fight for justice will enter its 40th year.

Mother was also a trooper as she stood up to racism and injustices. She taught her children the Bible and had shown them that Christianity was the right way to live.

As a young boy, I remember seeing several encounters my mother had with the racist. I remember being afraid for my mother, even though I felt like my mom wasn't afraid as she stood there and absorbed the abuse from the racist beast.

Mom's last encounter in Mississippi was with our plantation owner. He threatened to hunt her down like a dog and kill her if she lied to him as he questioned her about the whereabouts of my oldest brother. The vigilantes were hunting for him, wanting and waiting to lynch him for what they perceived were violations of their codes and rules or law.

As this racist threatened my mother, I clearly remember looking into his cold blue eyes and mom just sat there but mom was sure to answer him with "yes sir" and "no sir". I know for a fact that I was more afraid of this vulture than my mother was. The beast wore his gun and displayed it like he was the arm of the law. What the beast did not know is that mom had a 38 special on her and if need be I know she would have used it. Mom secretly held on to the pistol unbeknownst to the beast, she carried it most everywhere.

Mom knew exactly where my oldest brother was, but she looked the beast into those steel blue eyes and held to her answer, "No sir, I don't know where he is." Mom repeated that answer over and over and over again.

The beast threatened and cursed her for quite some time before he allowed us to leave his plantation. I observed all of this activity from the back of a flat bed Chevy while looking down at the vulture who was causing mother all this pain and grief.

As I laid in a jail cell locked up behind the wall of the most secure prison in Missouri, the sound of the steel bars still rattle in my mind as my cell door flew open and the prison guard yelled, "Little! You have a visitor!"

I was excited that someone had come to see me, because I felt very alone and confused, but determined to fight as I hurried up to the visitors room wondering who on earth was in there waiting to see me.

When I got to the visitors room, there sat my mother sitting there with open arms praying that we'll have another chance in freedom, to visit and to pray together. My mother was an avid believer in the Lord. She would not enter a room without blessing it or even putting food into her mouth before she blessed it as well. Everything had to be blessed or else mother would have no part of it.

Upon seeing mother, my immediate thoughts were of how she had traveled across the state to end up there having no car or drivers license. So I asked her, "Beatrice, how did you get here?" Mom told me that she took the Greyhound bus from Kansas City to Jefferson City, at Jefferson City she took a taxi cab to the agape house where she spent the night, then got up early and now here she is.

I was embarrassed that mother had gone through so much trouble to come see me. I was somewhat relieved because when I asked her how she had gotten here, in my mind, all I could see was someone waiting on mother in the hot car out in the parking lot. Her trip there was even more adventurous than that as she also had my sister's preschool twin boys tagging along, holding each one by a hand.

My mother had reared all of her own children into adulthood by now, but she had taken on a new responsibility of raising my sister's children. Her house was even busier now than when she had a houseful of her own. That was always her own choice, because mother loved her children, grandchildren, and great-grandchildren. Beatrice loved all children. They always held a special place in her heart.

As I sat there visiting with my mother that day, the temperature exceeded 100 degrees. In that room, my mother took a prison ministry trifold piece of paper and made herself a fan to stir up cool air. The hotter it got, the harder mom flopped that little fan as the little boys each stood up in their chairs and moved their faces closer in to mother's face, each trying to catch some of the coolness of the fan.

Mom was flopping that little fan around so hard, I could feel its coolness sitting across the table from her. It was a noticeable relief. As the little boys' faces were at each side of mom flopping that fan, every now and then mom would accidentally smack the faces of one of the little boys, and yes, I was keeping count. She smacked one boy five times and the other boy twice. I guarantee you, it was hotter than a two dollar pistol in there.

The prison visiting room was air conditioned but on this day it was broken. We all sat there and watched the temperature rise as the temperature climbed up towards 90 degrees and headed up to 100 degrees.

As we concluded our visit, I heard mother say to me in that old familiar voice, "Here, son, take this back there with you."

I looked at her hand thinking my mother had brought in some kind of contraband, but I really knew better than that. It was that piece of paper she'd been flopping around the whole visit. She slid it across the table towards me.

As mom waited on me to get to the visitors room, she had read that pamphlet and when she slid it across the table towards me, she probably felt like she was passing me some protection. In fact, she was. It was the word of the Lord and the shield that helped and guided me through the most violent period I could have ever encountered.

I looked at the piece of paper and it contained Bible scriptures and verses. I took the paper back to my jail cell and once there, I placed it in the Bible I'd been given by a prison minister, Rev. Kenny Foster.

I became familiar with Rev. Foster while in the visiting room and with Rev. Foster's fellowship tied with my mother's fellowship we developed through the postal, I became an avid faith partner and worshipper of Christ. Not that I didn't already believe in Jesus Christ, mom had already made sure I did, but now I was a lot more serious in my worship. Rev. Foster also became my prison barber. Rev. Foster spend as much time out of the jail cell as he did in it.

What neither Rev. Foster nor I realized at the time

was that Rev. Foster would eventually officiate the wedding of my future boss. My boss and I became really good friends because at the factory I was an asset to him by taking such a load off of him with my skills. When the boss told me where he was from, I asked him, "Do you know a Rev. Kenny Foster?" He said, "I should know him. He's the one who married me and my wife."

While I was confined, it was my relationship developed with Christ that helped me survive this miscarriage of justice. The seed of God had already been planted in me, thanks to the love and grace of my mother who made it a law in her family that each and every one of her children knew Christ Jesus before they ever left home. My mother had been handed the gift of the Lord from her mother who got it from her mother and I'm sure that goes all the way back to the day He rose.

When my mother passed away, I pulled out my old Bible and there was that piece of paper again. In my mind I could hear my mother's voice saying, "Here, take this with you" some 37 years earlier.

It had been over 37 years since mom passed that paper to me. The little pamphlet was frail and fading brown now. As I carefully unfolded the paper, this time I read the words within.

The pamphlet spoke about the right way to enter the kingdom of heaven and at my mother's funeral, I shared the pamphlet with the congregation.

The congregation enjoyed the message. It was perfect and it fit the situation exactly right. My tribute to mother didn't end there, as I told the patrons about the celebration of this person's homecoming. I told them that every night, my mother the Saint Beatrice would gather up her children around her bed, and we ended our day in fellowship with the Lord as we recited Matthew 6:9-13, the Lord's Prayer.

Every morning, the first thing we did was gather around the kitchen table. It was Matthew 6:9-13. Our Father who art in heaven.

If the Saint Beatrice called on you to lead the prayer you'd better be ready because Beatrice was a teacher. Beatrice was a preacher. Now, Beatrice is a child of God.

Beatrice let her children joke and play around a lot, but when the conversation was about Jesus, she allowed no room for nonsense. She would "beat the devil out of you: as she put it.

I remember the Saint Beatrice backhanding one of my brothers who made a joke when it came his turn to say his grace while we prepared to dine at the kitchen table. He said, "Oh I forgot, Jesus wept fell out the back door step". . . Boom!! No one ever tried that again. At least not within the sound of the Saint Beatrice.

But this verse resonated with Beatrice more than any other – Genesis 1:28, "God blessed them, and God said unto them, Be fruitful and multiply, and replenish the earth, and subdue it: and have dominion over the fish of the sea, and over the fowl of the air, and over every living thing that moveth upon the earth."

The Saint Beatrice did so help replenish this earth with 16 children, about 75 grandchildren, and over 75 and growing great-grandchildren. The Saint Beatrice was so lucky as to celebrate life with her great-great-grand-children.

In my mind I could see my grandmother Lillie Mae as if she was sitting right there right next to me. In her arms she's holding a baby child, it's the baby child Beatrice. And sitting there right next to my grandmother Lillie Mae is her momma my great-grandma Mother Becky, and sitting there next to my great-grandma Mother Becky is her momma my great-great-grandma Maggie. Having been freed from the bondage of slavery through the Emancipation Proclamation, my great-great-grandma Maggie picks up the baby child Beatrice and then she says, "We are free at last, we free at last, thank God almighty we's free at last." Then she says, "This child is Bound for Glory!!!"

John 3:3: Except a man be born again, he cannot see the Kingdom of God.

Luke 23:34: Then said Jesus, Father forgive them for they know now what they do.

Matthew 7:7: Ask and it shall be given you, seek and ye shall find, knock and it shall be open to you.

Those were the very first three verses that the Saint Beatrice sent me in our fellowship through the mail. I thought it was so fitting to share them at her funeral.

In the summer of 2014, the Saint Beatrice fell down as a result of the scorching summer heat we were having. She never walked on her own again. Because of that, mom was placed in a nursing home and had to be cared for almost as if she was an infant child.

After much controversy and confusion, the Saint

Beatrice ended up in a nursing home close to me. It was then that I took it in my own hands to make sure that she got the care and attention that she deserved.

I suddenly had a new full time job as I got up at 6:00am, took care of responsibilities around my home, before I drove the half hour drive up to the nursing home. It's a blessing that I was there because if I wouldn't have been, my mom wouldn't have lived those last three years I got to share with her.

This was the period before the COVID-19 era. It was a time that you could come and go into the nursing home as you pleased. I made it my duty to be at that place as soon as they unlocked the door to visitors at 7:00am.

The Saint Beatrice was closing toward 90 years old now. There were some days that she didn't even recognize me, but I didn't let that keep me away. I still showed up each day to make sure she got cleaned and fed. If there was a day that I didn't make it up there, I could tell when I saw her again as the employees of the home only did what they had to do in so many situations.

As I sat with mom one morning, she had a stroke right as we talked and was rushed away to a hospital.

For two weeks, I showed up at that hospital and hand fed mom her breakfast. I hastened her recovery and she was released back to the nursing home after about two weeks.

For some time after her release from the hospital, mom wouldn't eat unless I hand fed her, but if it was a food she really liked, she would eat it on her own. One food she wouldn't eat if she starved was powdered eggs. She'd had enough of them and if there were eggs on her plate she would ask, "Are those powdered eggs?" I tried to feed them to her several times to see if she could tell the difference. One bite was all it took. Yes, she could definitely tell the difference.

I took this special time visiting my mom picking out old memories and trying to make her remember anything I could get out of her. This was a special time for me to be with her and I enjoyed every second I got to be with her.

There were plenty of times that she would stare at me and say "Who are you and what do you want with me?" I'd turn these moments into sessions of recuperation making her talk, remember or questioning her about her current conditions. Do you recall this? Can you remember that? How do you feel today? Does it hurt anywhere on your body today? Probably the most unusual answer she gave me was when I would ask her who the president of the United States was. She'd answer "Roosevelt" every time. Mind you, this was 2014-2017.

Lots of days it would be approaching toward lunch and I'd spent the first half of our day out in the nursing home courtyard, sitting under a shade tree just talking.

Most of my mom's conversations were about getting up out of there. I'm positive that she would have walked away if she could have. This place reminded me of prison and for mom I'm sure it was.

One of the hardest periods I witnessed during this era was watching my mom bury her oldest daughter. She never really got over that and afterwards she'd often ask about her as if she was still alive.

There were times that she didn't remember me, but she never forgot about my sister's twin boys. She'd often say, "Hey, looky there, there goes Casey or is that Corey over there." It pained me so bad that neither one of those boys ever came to St. Louis to see her. She had taken those boys and raised them up as if they were her very own. She got over that though because I was there for her.

Those last three years were hard for me, because I witnessed this powerful black woman deteriorate and wither away being ravished by Alzheimers and several other illnesses before she had given this life all she had.

I kept mom on this side of the state in St. Louis for quite some time before I gave in. I allowed her to transfer to Kansas City where she spent the last six months with her daughters and grandchildren, including her beloved twin grandsons, Casey and Corey. I don't know how often those boys visited with my mom in those last six months, but if they would've known how much she loved them, I believe they would have given her as much time and attention as I did.

My wife and I traveled to Kansas City often during that last six months. I'm proud to say that none of Beatrice's children gave her more time and support during those last three years than did I. But each and every day I walked into those hospitals or nursing homes to see my mother, I was reminded of my days of incarceration. I could hear the prison bars rattling and the prison guard yelling out, "Little!! You have a visitor!" Those are the words I'd like to greet her with when I see her in heaven but maybe instead, "Hey there, Saint Beatrice, I'm not just a visitor here today. I'm home to stay."

On May 4, 2017, the Saint Beatrice was received into heaven. It is now her permanent place of residence.

When Beatrice entered into the kingdom, she was greeted with, "Job well done, my faithful servant."

Let your sorrow fade because Beatrice is now in the Kingdom. Even though there is great sorrow for Bea, there is no more pain.

Rest in peace, dear mother, this fight, this struggle and this battle is for you. Thank you for your guiding light and for your strong vision.

What you left me here on earth is something all the money in the world can't buy, the gift of the Holy Spirit and for that I am most thankful.

God bless you, Beatrice, you're truly a saint.

And God bless the United States of America.

www.ingramcontent.com/pod-product-compliance
Lightning Source LLC
Chambersburg PA
CBHW020947230426
43666CB00005B/202